COVID-19 And The American Phoenix

Dr. Miklos K. Radvanyi

Table of Contents

I. Troubled World

The turbulent two decades of the 21st century will surely remain a completely unsolvable riddle as long as the real impacts of the sudden collapse of the Soviet Union as well as the accompanying termination of the so-called Cold War between 1989 and 1991 are not understood correctly. Pursuant to the prevalent view in the United States of America, the breakup of the Soviet Union was the result of the inferiority of the Marxist-Leninist ideology as a functioning political, economic and social regime vis-a-vis the Western political culture. From the Kremlin's perspective, the United States of America and its allies, especially in Europe, had precious little to do with the demise of the Soviet Union. According to the Russian narrative, the Soviet Union was destroyed by the elite from within. A fundamental contradiction that is at the heart of the historic confusion of the last three decades. On the one hand, there is the image of the triumphant West. On the other hand, there is the picture of a completely defeated East. Consequently, what appeared to be a decisive victory over the "Evil Empire" from Washington was seen as a voluntary abandonment of the Cold War in Moscow.

The new Russia clearly looked for its place in the changing world. In order to be integrated into the just emerging new world order, its government, headed by an emotionally unstable alcoholic Boris Nikolayevich Yeltsin, was willing to accept Washington's lead. However, the imposition of democracy and free market economy have run into the impenetrable twin walls of the ossified mentality of the old communist bureaucracy and the all pervasive corruption that have plagued and rotted Russian societies to their core, starting in the early 13th century, from the onset of the Mongol rule in the Kievan Rus. Thus, the last decade of the 20th century proved that it is easier to erase the Soviet Union with its quasi-Communist ideology from the Russian minds than to change the ancestral mentality of the majority of the Russian people. Neither the Russian politicians nor the political leaders in the West fully comprehended at that time that it is not enough to defeat an entrenched and counterproductive political system. In order to change the minds of the people, the entire culture of a nation must be transformed. For this reason, the people should have been involved and should have been made a part of the great political, economic, social, and cultural transformation. Clearly, non participation creates confusion, misunderstanding, apathy, cynicism, and rejection. In one word, it leads to failure.

On the other side of the globe, President George H.W. Bush attempted to balance two seemingly contradictory visions. In order to strengthen the cohesion of the "Free World", he declared the vision of "Europe whole and free." In his speech on May 31, 1989, in Mainz, Germany, he assured the crowd that the United States of America is ready and willing to lead a united Europe based on the shared values of democracy, freedom, and prosperity.

Since it was impossible to establish a united Europe without the cooperation of the then Soviet Union, President Bush sat down on December, 2, 1989, off the coast of Malta, with the then Soviet leader Mikhail Sergeyevich Gorbachev. The Malta Summit officially put an end to the Cold War. However, beyond the declaratory good intentions of striving to build a new relationship between East and West, very little of strategic value was accomplished at Malta. In fact, President Bush's hybrid approach of providing American leadership in the post-Cold War world has proven to be wrong. Adapted also by his successor, President William J. (Bill) Clinton, this solution has not eliminated the old conflict between the dominant European power in the east and the rest of the continent in the west. On the contrary, with the emergence of the new Russian President Vladimir Vladimirovich Putin at the end of the century, this dualistic solution merely aggravated the confrontation between the less developed eastern and the more developed western parts of Europe.

Adding strategic insult to foreign policy incompetence by the Clinton Administration, President Clinton stated that his administration would use the so-called "peace dividend from the end of the Cold War" to enhance domestic spending, mainly in the health and social security areas of the economy. Concurrently, the Clinton Administration completely failed to formulate a coherent global foreign policy and to set national strategic objectives for the present and the future. No wonder then that under these forlorn conditions American foreign policy was not coordinated by either the White House or the State Department. Instead, foreign policy was franchised haphazardly to several departments, various congressional committees, and even the institutions of higher education such as Harvard, Yale, Princeton, Stanford, etc. In particular the latter did become very active in filling the foreign policy vacuum in Washington D.C. Loaded at that time with so-called "Russia experts" who arrived in great numbers from the former Soviet Union, they spotted an opportunity to join the party in the new Russian Federation and try to enrich their universities and themselves by the Russian version of "Wild West Capitalism." Simultaneously, NATO's national security strategy remained frozen in the obsolete goal of old fashioned containment and the dead end doctrine of Mutually Assured Destruction (MAD).

In the meantime, both states faced major domestic and foreign policy challenges. Moscow had to manage the international aftermath of the dissolution of the Soviet Union and the withdrawal of its troops from Eastern Europe and Afghanistan. Domestically, the reorganization of the government and the ensuing chaos as well as the heavy losses inflicted by the robber economy paved the way for the emergence of a new strongman in the Kremlin at the end of 1999. The history of the successive two decades under President-Prime Minister-and again President Putin has contained more failures than successes. The Russian Federation is still a developing country waiting to progress. The form of government has reverted to outright dictatorship, the economy has continued being dependent on the export of raw materials, and the pervasiveness of corruption as well as the degree of the people's immorality have remained legendary. The arrival in massive lethal force of COVID-19 to Russia has shown the Russian people and the rest of the world that President Putin is far from being the superman depicted in so many staged photographs. Spoiling mightily the 75th anniversary of the Soviet Union's victory against Hitler's Germany in what the Russians call the Great Patriotic War, the novel coronavirus has been running literally unchecked by the authorities. To underscore the historically "all-to-familiar" Russian incompetence, hospitals are burning and medics who spoke out against the abysmal conditions in the health industry mysteriously fell from high windows to their untimely deaths. Meanwhile, President Putin has been hiding in his heavily guarded Novo-Ogaryovo compound outside Moscow. His rare appearances have only occurred via the electronic media.

Clearly, the "new Russia" has proved to be the reproduction of the old despotic Tsarist Imperial Russia and the Soviet Union. Presently, the Russian Federation with President Putin at the helm is a military despotism par excellence, devoid of liberty, tolerance and humanism. As previously, the masses are enslaved and are kept by the government propaganda as close as possible to mental imbecility. The dread of the people is matched step by step by the fear of the President and his entourage. This horrible mutual fearfulness increases exponentially with the rise of oppression and the corresponding rebelliousness of the people. Thus, instead of progressing toward democracy, Russia will remain a despotic state that will continue to pose an enduring military threat to the rest of Europe and the United States of America.

In foreign policy, President Putin's megalomania and hubris have created more problems than solutions. It is safe to predict that his artificial cooperation with Iran and Turkey in Syria will end in a violent fiasco. His newfound fondness for the People's Republic of China will surely end in disappointment, if not in a catastrophe. His meddling in Ukraine has already put him in a lose-lose situation. His contradictory policies vis-a-vis Europe have only confused and alienated the governments in the continent. To summarize it, the upshot of Russia's overall condition and the effects of President Putin's policies have been counterproductive for the domestic as well as the foreign integrity of the Russian Federation, because both have contributed to the decay of stability and peace regionally as well as globally.

In Washington, the lackluster performance of the Clinton Administration, the terrorist attacks of September 11, 2001, the resulting twin invasion of Afghanistan and Iraq, the financial crisis of the last two years of the first decade, and the general mediocrity of the Bush presidency, followed by the glaring professional incompetence and the moral ambiguity of the Obama Administration, combined to weaken the stability and peace upon which the post World War II international system was founded.

Domestically, American society has regressed into the Obama Administration's deliberately induced and revoltingly atrocious political, ethnic, economic, religious, and race-based divisions. The over politicization of every aspects of American society has lead to the sudden emergence of all kinds of movements, such as #Black Lives Matter, the Tea Party, # Me Too, Antifa, and various partisan groups espousing divergent political and social causes, such as gun control, climate change, illegal immigration, privacy rights, abortion, and the overreach of the judiciary, among others. Yet, none of these movements and groups have been intellectually thoughtful or sincere. Hastily improvised by the least educated and most excitable elements of American society, mostly with scant educational background, but strongly incited by the Obama Administration with its slogan of "fundamental transformation", and an irresponsible media, Americans have become increasingly less confident and more skeptical of their government's ability to manage the domestic and foreign challenges facing their nation. Lawlessness as the driving force of change at all cost has become the great passion that, combined with the ugly charge of racism, have put the nation into many artificially induced crises. Running for president with the frightening promise of continuing the Obama chaos and nonsense on the Democrat ticket, Hillary R. Clinton was soundly defeated in November 2016, by the Republican Donald J. Trump, an outsider. The events that have immediately followed the election of the latter will enter the annals of American history as perhaps the vilest conspiracy against the constitutional order of the United States of America.

The colossal enormity of the plan to delegitimize by the use of unquestionably illegal means, including absolute lies and blatant innuendos, the Republican presidential nominee and his campaign could have been originated only at the highest level in the White House. Regardless whether the core idea was conceived by former President Barack H. Obama personally, his responsibility, as the constitutional head of the Executive Branch, is beyond any doubt. Moreover, he had a very personal ax to grind against Donald J. Trump who publicly questioned the former president's eligibility to the highest elected office of the United States of America.

Beyond the moral qualms about pursuing his personal vendetta to the detriment of national security, President Obama deliberately exacerbated every interaction between the Democrats and Republicans by reducing his hatred toward President Trump to the simplistic notion of "us" versus "them." Moreover, the former's toxic politics of relativity has also intimated that the supporters of the new president must only be defined in relation to the enlightened and virtuous Obama Democrats. As Hillary Clinton stated during her failed campaign, those who opposed her agenda were "deplorables." Thus having preemptively destroyed any possibility of nonpartisan unifying ideas and actions, President Obama, while still in office, embarked on destroying the principle of the rule of law too. Finally, in his fundamental arrogance and hatred, he undoubtedly attempted to paralyze the incoming Trump Administration for years to come domestically as well as internationally. Consequently, "Trump bashing" has become both a national and international pastime for all the "America critics and haters."

The insinuation that the Republican nominee beat the Democrat nominee, because the incoming president and his advisors "colluded" with the Russian turned out to be totally unfounded, essentially a hoax concocted by the White House and carried out by the former president's loyal followers, namely, Ben Rhodes, Susan Rice, Samantha Power, John Brennan, James Clapper, Loretta Lynch, Sally Yates, James Comey, Andrew McCabe, and countless other underlings. In the absence of a strong Attorney General who recused himself, his deputy Rod Rosenstein ran the show. The ensuing illegal Mueller investigation did produce zero incriminating evidence. The follow-up impeachment process by the House of Representatives and the trial in the Senate ended in a total embarrassment for the Pelosi-Schiff-Nadler triumvirate. Their accomplices, the overwhelming majority of the highly partisan media have been fatally discredited.

Yet the real victim of the weaponization of political differences has been the United States of America and its relationships with the rest of the world. Specifically, President Putin must have concluded that America has become woefully unbalanced. In view of the upcoming elections in November, the situation specifically in Europe and the Middle East will surely become exceedingly complex and thus alarmingly more complicated. The pandemic caused by COVID-19 has added another major factor to the already existing disorder in a troubled world.

II. COVID-19 And The China Question

On January 15, 2020, a man of Chinese descent and a US resident in his 30s, arrived in Seattle from Wuhan. Immediately after his landing, he was admitted to Providence Regional Medical Centre Everett. According to a local health officer by the name of Chris Bitters, the patient was "in good condition and hospitalized out of an abundance of precaution and for short-term monitoring." As an afterthought he added: "He reported that he did not visit any of those implicated markets in Wuhan (referring to the so-called Wet Markets) and did not know anyone that was ill. He was just travelling from that area." The announcement was followed by the CDC's assessment, according to which this known first case's risk to the general public is "low" because he was admitted to the hospital early and had been "very cooperative" with health authorities. Washington State Secretary of Health John Wiesman doubled down on praising the Chinese man thus: "I'm grateful that the man who tested positive for the virus acted so quickly to seek treatment. Because of that we were able to isolate him away from the public, and these actions gave us a head start….All this work means that we believe the risk to the public is low." Uh-Oh! Mindless political correctness in full display by bureaucratic naivete and incompetence, with its potentially destructive character.

On January 11, 2020, just four days before the Chinese citizen's arrival in Seattle, Chinese officials reported that the total number of "confirmed" cases have jumped to 324, the bulk of them in the epicenter and ground zero of the COVID-19 epidemic, in Hubei province. Additional confirmed cases were reported in quick succession in Beijing, Shanghai, Tianjin, Guangdong, Zhejiang, Henan and Chongqing. Concomitantly, Wuhan health authorities admitted that 15 medical personnel in the city have contracted the virus, an indirect confirmation that the virus was spreading by human transmission.

Meanwhile, a study funded by a British Academy Leverhulme Small Research Grant about the degree of honesty found that the most dishonest are the Chinese and the most honest are the British and Japanese people. According to the South China Morning Post, in the first test, 1,500 participants from 15 countries were asked to flip a coin and state whether it landed on "heads" or "tails." The participants were told that in case the coin lands on "heads", they would be rewarded with $3 to $5. Participants from mainland China were found to be the most dishonest, with 70% estimated to have lied about which side the coins landed on, compared to 3.4% of British participants. The second test was composed of a music quiz, in which the participants were told that if they answered all questions correctly they would be rewarded financially. However, they had to state that they did not search for answers on the internet. Here, Japanese and British were judged to be the most honest and Turkish and Chinese the least forthcoming. Finally, participants were also asked to rate the average honesty of their respective countrymen. As a result, the participants were most critical toward their own people. As the Romans claimed: "Veritas liberabit vos." "The truth shall liberate you."

It is also a primordial truth that nations down on their luck in the present always proudly wallow in their glorious past. The People's Republic of China is no exception. Although reality almost always clashes with the legendary, Chinese propaganda blares in unison that the five or three thousand years of the Han people's history is full of heroes who committed unimaginably benevolent acts, sage geniuses whose insights and wisdoms are unparalleled in human history, and leaders whose visions and foresights have guided them from one bright zenith to ever more perfect summits. Of course, nothing is further from the truth.

As a whole, Chinese history is a lesson in elementary despotism that has only brought for the China of today limited developments. The People's Republic of China, when stripped of the outward facade of busting cities, a thin layer of a middle class, and impressive infrastructure, which seem to be varnished and modern, does not differ essentially by its mentality from Imperial China of the Middle Ages. Indeed, Mao Zedong's 1949 version of Communism was nothing but a belated attempt to resuscitate the moribund system of Imperial China by an even stricter despotism. For this reason, the basic traits of the Chinese people are still what they were three thousand, one thousand, five hundred, and fifty years ago.

Throughout millenia and countless centuries, the enduring complaints of both Chinese and foreigners have been the dishonesty of the people in general and their shameless cheating in dealings with other people, be it in business or production of goods. From time immemorial, Chinese traders have customarily put fraudulent brands and fake trademarks on their merchandise, deception has gone hand-in-hand with inferior quality, bribery has been as common as lying, and schools have taught from the start that cheating on the "hairy people", meaning all non Han Chinese, is a virtue and should be a source of pride, because those people deserve to be disrespected on the account of their inferiority to the racially superior Chinese nation.

These abysmal Chinese practices have been in full display throughout the COVID-19 pandemic. In addition to hoarding and then mislabeling various personal protection equipment (PPE) from all over the world, European countries have discovered that masks supplied by China for inflated prices had little or no protective properties at all. The same has applied to rapid test kits. Countries that have ordered do-it-yourself pinprick antibody tests have not fared better. The same fate has awaited the N95 respirators, ventilators, and other similar medical supplies. Clearly, human lives mean nothing to the Chinese government and its licensed mercenaries when it comes to generating income by defrauding the gullible foreigners.

Instead of supplying quality merchandise, the Chinese Government has mounted a humanitarian aid Blitz to counter international criticism of its outrageous and hypocritical trade practices. An army of Chinese government spokespersons, headed by Zhao Lijian, a foreign ministry spokesman, have arrogantly criticized everybody who dared question the sincerity and integrity of the Chinese Communist Party, the Chinese authorities, and their licensed or unlicensed distributors. The Chinese pushback has been coordinated centrally and has been well financed. Beijing's investments in its foreign media presence have been relentless and enormous. From the written to the electronic media, the Chinese propaganda machine has produced slick videos and sophisticated editorials. Calling objective and factual reporting "immoral slanders," they have pointed out the alleged political motivations of the critics, while blaming officials in the rest of the world who "ignored early warnings" of the pandemic. The narrative of "shifting the blame" has become the focal point of Chinese disinformation.

Having been brought up to lying, cheating, and racist mentality, Chinese have sucked in this unique combination of immoral traits with their mothers' milk. Even more alarmingly, they have seen these traits by watching their fathers, grandfathers, great grandfathers, and by having listened to tales about the long lines of their equally dishonest ancestors. To add insult to injury, the Chinese Communist Party controlled education system, the media, the government, all have conspired to poison the minds of every citizen to think that the current total surveillance despotism is designed to make them happy and prosperous and, therefore, the best form of government in the world. Again, a Roman proverb comes to mind: "Rustici Fusistis et Estis." "You still remain what you were before."

These quintessential Chinese characteristics have been projected onto Beijing's foreign policy too. In the main, the Chinese Communist Party and the government have not been searching for allies or alliances. They have been looking for states whose leaders could be corrupted and rendered totally subservient to Chinese foreign policy by making them hopelessly addicted to and dependent on Chinese financial and economic assistance. In Asia, the People's Republic has assumed the role of a ruthless bully, especially in the South China Sea. In Africa, the strategy of corrupting politicians has found ample number of receptive takers. In the European continent, particularly in Central and Eastern Europe, the Balkans, Italy, France and Spain, Beijing has pursued a cautious financial and economic penetration strategy. Contrary to Russian objectives aimed at weakening or even splitting up the European Union, the People's Republic's goal is to gradually erode the close relationships between the United States of America and its allies. Yet, Beijing's imperial ambitions have not stopped on the bilateral level. Beijing's corrupt practices have also poisoned the orderly functioning of the United Nations and almost all of its specialized agencies. The best and most recent illustration is the World Health Organization's (WHO) dysfunctional reaction to the outbreak of the CODIV-19 in Wuhan, China.

Its current Director General Dr. Tedros Adhanom Ghebreyesus, less an Ethiopian microbiologist and more a dedicated anti-democratic and anti-capitalist, Marxist politician, flew to Beijing on January 28, 2020, almost a month after the Chinese physician Li Wenliang warned his colleagues and the larger public about the outbreak of an illness resembling severe acute respiratory syndrome (SARS), which sparked the previous pandemic in 2003. For his professional insight Dr. Li was summoned by the Public Security Bureau in Wuhan, which accused him of having made false statements and thus disrupting public order. He died, while many of his colleagues were arrested, interrogated, and harassed for speaking out against the politically motivated ignorance of the Chinese Communist Party. In spite of a loud chorus of more Chinese physicians, that the virus was spreading between humans, the WHO issued a statement on January 14, 2020, declaring that there was "no clear evidence of human-to-human transmission of the novel coronavirus." Even as late as January 20, 2020, ABC quoted WHO as stating that there was "limited human-to-human transmission" of the coronavirus. For good measure the WHO announcement added the following sentence: "This is in line with experience with other respiratory illnesses and in particular with other coronavirus outbreaks." The WHO finally declared the coronavirus a global emergency only on January 30, 2020.

As a countermeasure, President Trump froze U.S. funding for the WHO. In his reasoning he criticized the irresponsible behavior of the WHO. "The World Health Organization has been a disaster. Everything they've said was wrong. And they're China-centric. They agree with China, whatever China wants to do. So our country, perhaps foolishly in retrospect, has been paying $450 million a year to the World Health Organization. And China's been paying $38 million a year. According to the May 8, 2020, edition of the German magazine Der Spiegel that based its article on a report by the German intelligence agency Bundesnachrichtendienst (BDN), this statement was designed to conceal the spread of the coronavirus upon the explicit personal request of President Xi whose wife Peng Liyuan happens to be a Goodwill Ambassador to the World Health Organization. Naturally, her connection to the Chinese supreme leader is not mentioned in the organization's website. There she is listed deferentially as Ms. Peng who is a singing star in China. The Der Spiegel article claims that President Xi personally called Dr. Tedros and requested that the latter and the WHO should refrain from declaring that COVID-19 could be transmitted among humans. Moreover, Taiwan News also reported that President Xi asked Dr. Tedros to stop a declaration by the WHO of a pandemic. Commensurately, India World reported on April 30, 2020, that the Chinese government locked down all domestic traffic internally by the end of January 2020 but did not stop international flights from leaving Chinese cities at least until the end of March. The paper also provided a chronology of the gradual lockdown that clearly showed the Chinese leadership's nefarious intent. Elevating China's boundless chutzpah to new heights, its vice-minister for foreign affairs Qin Gang called in Italy's ambassador to Beijing Luca Ferrari following the installation of Rome's flight ban vis-a-vis all Chinese carriers and complained about the one-sided Italian measures. The former termed Italy's decision to stop all flights "unacceptable," because "Many Chinese are still stranded in Italy." The rest of the story is well-known. The city of Milan in northern Italy and the entire Lombardy region have become the epicenter of the COVID-19 pandemic throughout the central and southern parts of Europe. Again, Dr. Tedros and WHO slavishly followed and fully supported Beijing's disinformation campaign.

Along the same line, Al Arabiya published an article on April 9, 2020, claiming that international flights from and to China, especially to Hubei province were not stopped until March 27, 2020. Under the title "Coronavirus: Critics ask why China allowed flights out of Hubei during outbreak" was a damning indictment of the Chinese Communist Party and its government.

Feeling the heat of ubiquitous international outrage, the WHO recently changed its tune and blamed the Chinese Communist Party for intentionally withholding pertinent information concerning COVID-19 from the organization. As the Associated Press reported on June 2, 2020, Maria Van Kerkhove, an epidemiologist for the WHO, complained that she and her colleagues received the needed information to assess the nature of the novel coronavirus and their response to it from the Chinese authorities in January in a substantially delayed timeframe.

Together, these actions by President Xi indisputably point to his and his party's strategic intention to spread the novel coronavirus and thus to ensure that the People's Republic of China would not be the only country that would suffer significant political, financial, and economic hardships. True to its dishonest operating tradition under the leadership of Dr. Tedros, the WHO vehemently denied the accuracy of the Der Spiegel article: "Der Spiegel reports of a January 21, 2020, telephone conversation between WHO Director-General Dr. Tedros Adhanom Ghebreyesus and President Xi Jinping of China are unfounded and untrue." The statement continued thus: "Dr. Tedros and President Xi did not speak on 21st of January and they have never spoken by telephone. Such inaccurate reports distract and detract from WHO's and the world's efforts to end the COVID-19 pandemic."

To echo the WHO, the People's Republic's Ministry of Foreign Affairs published a belated article on COVID-19 and China on May 10, 2020. In this article the Foreign Ministry attempted to dispute in 24 point "24 lies coming out of the U.S. over COVID-19." From arguing against calling the novel coronavirus the "Chinese virus" or "Wuhan virus," to defending the work and integrity of the Wuhan Institute of Virology, and labeling the existence of wet markets a "western myth," the Chinese authorities have again demonstrated the extent of their troubled relations with the facts and the truth.

Later, in Beijing, after meeting with President Xi, the newly enlightened Dr. Tedros praised Chinese authorities for "setting a new standard for outbreak control," lauding their "openness for sharing information." Subsequently, the same Dr. Tedros prevented the WHO from declaring an emergency over the objections of several emergency committee members. When he finally relented on January 30th, he did it with a big caveat by again praising China for "slowing the spread (of the coronavirus) to the rest of the world." Moreover, to demonstrate where his mind, heart, and pocket reside, he criticized President Trump's travel ban on January 31st by stating that it would "have the effect of increasing fear and stigma, with little public health benefit." Again, in its February report the WHO opined thus: "In the face of a previously unknown virus, China has rolled out perhaps the most ambitious, agile and aggressive disease containment effort in history." The same report sounded enthusiastic about China's "uncompromising and rigorous use of non-pharmaceutical measures" and Beijing's brilliant strategy that "demonstrated that containment can be adapted and successfully operationalized in a wide range of settings."

It is worthwhile to note that all these statements came from an incompetent and corrupt political hack and not a professional physician. Having been the first non-physician at the helm of WHO in the organization's long history, Dr. Tedros was, in a previous incarnation, part of an oppressive dictatorship that repeatedly lied about three consecutive cholera outbreaks in Ethiopia. As Ethiopia's foreign minister between 2012 and 2016, he defended the regime's egregious human rights violations and its genocidal actions in Ethiopia's largest region of Oromia in 2015, and the Amhara region in 2016. Clearly, the bells across the globe toll, with the exception of China, for Dr. Tedros. The demands for his resignation are absolutely justified. For the sake of global health and the future integrity of the WHO, he must go immediately. He must take full responsibility for his actions and statements. The buck must stop with the head of the organization. Both the world as well as the WHO deserve a dedicated professional and a real nonpartisan Director General.

The credibility of Dr. Tedros and the World Health Organization have been mortality damaged by the newest revelations that the U.N.-supported global health institution changed its COVID-19 timeline concerning its initial information about the pandemic. On June 29, 2020, the official website of the organization was revised. According to the new version, the "WHO's Country Office in the People's Republic of China picked up a media statement by the Wuhan Municipal Health Commission from their website on cases of 'viral pneumonia' in Wuhan, People's Republic of China." To add another self-inflicted insult to its incompetence injury, the website decided to dig an even deeper hole for its already tarnished reputation by adding that "the WHO's open-source intelligence platform also picked up a Chinese language news report from Finance Sina, a Chinese outlet, about the same cluster of cases in Wuhan, attributed to a 'pneumonia' of unknown causes."

Historically, corruption had been a destructive curse of all Chinese societies. Yet, with the establishment of the People's Republic of China in 1949, corruption, driven by the monopoly of the Chinese Communist Party and its leading members, has institutionalized lawlessness combined with the notion of political and legal impunity. Within this perfect storm, the abuse of power for personal ends has conquered all the institutions of government, including party and administrative organizations, law enforcement, healthcare, education, and business entities. The political thaw that followed Mao Zedong's death has only exacerbated the already existing destructive nature of the all encompassing corruption with "Chinese Characteristics," to paraphrase President Xi's favorite slogan. Deng Xiaoping's call to the Chinese people to enrich themselves irrespective of moral considerations, i.e. " it does not matter if a cat is black or white, so long as it catches mice," has been widely interpreted as an open invitation for Chinese Communist Party's sanctioned boundless corruption.

As long as Chinese corruption has remained within the boundaries of the People's Republic, it has only been a relatively well contained local phenomenon, which has not risen to a significant international problem. However, with the disappearance of the Soviet Union and the independence of its oppressed satellites the question of the quality of political and market liberalization has gained renewed importance for the United States of America as well as for its European allies. However, more freedom in the region has resulted in a marked increase in the levels of corruption. According to a 2019 report by Transparency International, Eastern Europe, which encompasses all of the previous states within the former Soviet sphere of influence, have experienced "limited separation of powers, abuse of state resources for electoral purposes," opaque political party financing, and conflicts of interest. Coupled with limited judicial independence, minimal press freedoms, and lack of checks and balances among the three branches of governments, these perfect storms have created a very similar kind of corruption that exists in the People's Republic of China of today.

In this context, the People's Republic has initiated the 16+1 platform, also called the China-Central and Eastern European Countries (China-CEEC) summit in 2012. Ostensibly, it has been designed to further economic cooperation between Beijing and a collection of 11 European Union (EU) member states and 5 Balkan countries, namely, Albania, Bosnia-Herzegovina, Bulgaria, Croatia, the Czech Republic, Estonia, Hungary, Latvia, Lithuania, Macedonia, Montenegro, Poland, Romania, Serbia, Slovakia, and Slovenia, the objectives of the initiative are devoid of politics, and thus sound fairly innocent. In its last gathering on April 11-12, 2019, in Zagreb, Croatia, no comprehensive economic strategies were discussed or agreed upon. While the establishment of the platform has predated the "Belt and Road Initiative" (BRI), China has viewed the 16+1 format as a vehicle to strengthen bilateral relations with the participating countries via investments in infrastructure and all kinds of technologies. Needless to say that corruption has been ripe concerning the $15.4 billion investment monies that have already been made available for those countries. Also not surprisingly, in countries that have received above average investment levels, corruption has risen exponentially. It should be noted too that EU officials in Brussels have been increasingly critical of the 16+1 format. Mainly, they are worried that China's real intentions are to undermine European unity in general, and skew European Union's policies across Europe in favor of the People's Republic of China in particular.

The impacts of Chinese corruption globally have been devastating, especially for the economies of developing countries. Fighting and rooting out Beijing's corrupting influence and designs internationally are essential for economic developments across the globe. Pursuant to a 2018 report by the United Nations (UN), worldwide corruption is estimated to cost at least $2.6 billion, or 5% of the global GDP. Beyond the economic, financial, and cultural damage, pervasive corruption also destroys those countries' progress toward developing genuinely democratic institutions. Therefore, decisive countering of Chinese corruption is essential. Beijing's strategy of buying up governments and politicians also in Africa, Central and South America, and South-East Asia could not stand, because it would only lead to a corrupt world ruled by the Chinese Communist Party and its Politburo.

As a clear confirmation of Chinese duplicity and an additional slap in the face of the international community and WHO, on May 15, 2020, Liu Dengfeng, a supervisor with China's National Health Commission, essentially a low level bureaucrat within the Chinese government, admitted that "the Chinese government issued an order on January 3rd to dispose of coronavirus samples" at unauthorized laboratories. As reported by Newsweek, Mr. Liu denied that the samples were terminated in order to conceal evidence. Rather, he claimed, it was done to comply with Chinese public health laws to "prevent risk to laboratory biological safety and prevent secondary disasters caused by unidentified pathogens." He also stated that the laboratories at issue were "unauthorized" to handle such samples.

Of course, his lame excuses and explanations beg the question - why was the Chinese government so confused about the identity of the new pathogen? If the pathogen was "unidentified," how could government authorities ascertain that it was so dangerous that it had to be destroyed immediately, without conducting any further research? Finally, if this new pathogen posed such a biological safety risk that it had to be eliminated, why did China conceal the existence and the destruction of the pathogen from the WHO until May 15, 2020, and lie about it incessantly?

According to an even more recent Harvard Medical School case study of early June 2020, analyzing satellite images indicate that "a dramatic increase" in the number of cars parked outside six major Wuhan hospitals in September 2019, with a peak in traffic in December 2019, were observed.

"Individual hospitals have days of high relative volume in both fall and winter 2019. However, between September and October 2019, five of the six hospitals show their highest relative daily volume of the analyzed series," the case study opined. In addition, the researchers also saw increased internet traffic on search terms relating to COVID-19-like symptoms, such as coughing and diarrhea, on the Chinese search engine Baidu. Dr. John Brownstein, the leader of the research team told ABC News: "Clearly, there was some level of social disruption taking place well before what was previously identified as the start of the novel coronavirus pandemic."

Obviously, China cannot credibly answer these questions. Continuing to lie is also not an option in the world of social media and high technology spying. While following the Nazi Joseph Goebels' dictum of repeating a lie often is enough to brandish it as the truth, President Xi and his government fell into a classic trap. The bubble of the illusion of truth burst and the leaders of the People's Republic were exposed as loathsome mini emperors without clothing. Although as the saying goes that hope springs eternal, a reasonable person would not bet his money on President Xi and his colleagues to learn their lessons from the COVID-19 fiasco. More likely that they would continue to bribe, to lie, to obfuscate, and to disseminate hateful propaganda, in order to advance their final solution of ruling the entire world.

But the most damning evidence came from a resident of the city of Wuhan by the name of Fang Fang who wrote a diary of the local coronavirus history in Wuhan. She published her diary in chronological increments on her blog between January 25, 2020, and March 24, 2020. Published on May 17, 2020, by the Sunday Times, Fang Fang revealed that her brother, a professor at Huazhong University of Science and Technology, told her that the virus was highly contagious and transferable among humans. She contrasted her brother's statement with the official propaganda that asserted the non contagious character of the novel coronavirus: "Not contagious between people; it's controllable and preventable." Fang Fang wrote in great details about the scramble for facemasks, food, and supplies, while hospitals all over the city of 11 million teetered on the brink of collapse.

Her February 13, 2020, entry described the chaotic conditions inside a local crematorium, illustrating the scenes with photographs taken by her friend and showing a "pile of mobile phones on the floor of a funeral home; the owners of those phones had already been reduced to ash." Other entries in Fang Fang's diary were full of horrific tales of desperate residents aged 3 to 80 who were left alone amidst the ubiquitous chaos to fend for themselves. Even more significantly, she noted that her physician friends knew from the beginning that there was a human-to-human transmission of the disease, which they reported to their superiors, without any noticeable results.

According to the Sunday Times, the full English version of her diary will go on sale on June 30, 2020, titled "Dispatches from a quarantined city: Wuhan Diary." Another publication in German is titled "Wuhan Diary: The forbidden diary from the city where the corona crisis began," has already drawn the ire of Chinese officials for its alleged "bad intentions."

Vividly illustrating the despotic nature of the regime, a campaign is already on its way to destroy her both intellectually as well as physically. Accused of being a "hanjian," meaning a "race traitor" to the Han Chinese, her life has been threatened. Stoking the flames of racial hatred, Hu Xijin, editor in chief of the ultranationalist tabloid Global Times wrote that the foreign publications of the diary "is not really in good taste."

Again, a Roman saying coined by Seneca comes to mind: "Veritas nunquam perit," the truth never perishes, even when it is killed from time to time. From the inception of Mao's despotism, the Chinese Communist Party has forced the people to lie and, simultaneously, actively deny the truth. Another great European who lived between the 18th and 19th centuries, Klemens Wenzel Nepomuk Lothar, Prince of Metternich-Winneburg zu Beilstein, analyzing the causes for the failure of the the French King Louis Philippe who ruled between 1830 and 1848, said in volume five of his Memories: "...condemned to hover between two realities, Monarchy and Republic, Louis Philippe is in a vacuum, for a lie is a vacuum."

In the case of the People's Republic of China, this version of Chinese despotism has also been founded on a lie; the lie that Maoism would bring the perfect utopia in the form of heavenly peace and stability to the Chinese people and the rest of the world. Instead, what four generations of Chinese people have gotten in reality were thus far indescribable sufferings, ubiquitous misery, devastating famines, and senseless political terror. Such a despotic regime is vulnerable and, therefore, cannot endure for long. Albeit outwardly it appears to be strong and stable, historically, no despotism based on total oppression had been able to maintain itself by sheer force. By demonstrating ruthless power at home and abroad, the Chinese Communist Party only attempts to conceal its fear from being challenged decisively and by an even more determined force. The world should realize that although the military, economic, and financial strength of the People's Republic are facts, they lack the solid political foundation that democracy provides the United States of America and many other states across the globe. For these reasons, the outcome of any future global confrontation would not favor a despotic China.

III. Frenzied Hysteria Or A Historic Crossroads In 21st Century Politics?

According to scientists, when an infectious, or communicable, disease remains within the boundaries of a single state, it is called an epidemic. However, when the disease crosses the boundaries of a single state, it is classified as a pandemic.

The earliest recorded epidemic was the plague of Athens during the second year of the Peloponnesian War in 430 BC. Most probably the combination of smallpox and typhus, the epidemic killed an estimated 75,000 to 100,000, including Pericles, the leader of Athens. It returned twice to wreak havoc on the population in 429 BC, and in the winter of 427-426 BC. Well documented by the historian Thucidides, this epidemic had significant effects on the city state as well as the subsequent outcome of the long war with Sparta.

The plague of Antonine in 165 A.D. was the first recorded pandemic. In all likelihood it was brought to Eastern and Central Europe by the marauding Huns via the German tribes, the smallpox virus infected the Roman troops who spread the virus throughout the Roman Empire. This pandemic endured until 180 A.D., also killing the Emperor Marcus Aurelius. The Antonine plague had no major effects on the Roman Empire.

The next known pandemic started in Ethiopia around 250 A.D., passed through Northern Africa as well as Carthage, and reached both Egypt and Rome. Called the Cyprian Plague after the Christian bishop of Carthage, it devastated the Mediterranean region for the next three centuries. Finally, in 444 A.D., it hit Britain and led ultimately to the Saxon invasion and occupation of the island.

This pandemic was followed by the Justinian bubonic plague in 541 A.D. Originated in Egypt, the plague spread through the entire Mediterranean, grievously affecting the entire Byzantine Empire. This pandemic definitely put an end to the Emperor's ambitions to unite the eastern and western parts of the Roman Empire together. Moreover, it caused heavy economic devastation throughout the Empire. Recurrences over the next two centuries killed an estimated 50 million people, approximately 26% of the then world population.

The second significant outbreak of the bubonic plague started in Asia and gradually moved westward with the caravans. It entered Europe through the Sicilian port of Messina in 1347 A.D. England and France were almost totally paralyzed by the pandemic. As a result, the British feudal system was destroyed by the economic and demographic changes that were due to the plague. Moreover, the pandemic brought about a truce to the war between England and France. Finally, the Vikings' expansion beyond Greenland toward North America came to a screeching halt.

In 1817, came the first of seven cholera pandemics that terrorized the world for the next 150 years. It originated in Russia where the cholera bacterium killed at least one million people. Through feces-infested waters and foods, the bacterium was carried by British soldiers to India where millions more perished. The global reach of the British Empire, especially its navy, carried the cholera bacterium to Spain, Africa, Indonesia, China, Japan, Italy, Germany, and the Americas. A vaccine that was available in 1885, only slowed but did not eradicate the cholera pandemic.

1855 saw the return of the dreaded bubonic pandemic. Again, beginning in Yunnan, China, it quickly moved to India and Hong Kong, killing at least 15 million people. Two rebellions in China erupted as a result, namely the Panthay rebellion, known to Chinese as the Du Wenxiu Rebellion, and the more enduring Taiping rebellion, also known to Chinese as the Taiping Civil War or the Taiping Revolution, which was waged from 1850 to 1864 between the established Manchu-led Qing dynasty and the Hakka-led Taiping Heavenly Kingdom.

The Fiji Measles in 1875, the Russian flu in 1889, and the 1918 Spanish flu pandemics followed in quick succession. Again, millions died across the globe.

The 1957 Asian flu pandemic again killed more than one million people, 116,000 in the United States of America alone. In this case, a vaccine was developed fairly quickly, effectively containing the further spread of the pandemic.

In 1981, the HIV/AIDS pandemic ravaged mainly the homosexual communities across the globe. Until various treatments have been developed, at least 35 million people died of the virus that originated in West Africa.

The Severe Acute Respiratory Syndrome or SARS outbreak of 2003, started in China and quickly spread to 26 other countries. Quarantine measures were fairly effective and the virus was contained within a year. At that time, China was criticized for suppressing information about the virus at the beginning of the outbreak.

The deceptions and contradictions that had been inherent in Chinese culture from time immemorial, have been on full display from the start of the newest pandemic, COVID-19. Although the first manifestations of the novel coronavirus cannot be determined with absolute certainty, the December 8, 2019 date, provided by the Chinese authorities, appears to be less than believable. According to other sources, the first registered case occurred sometime in mid-November when a female patient showed SARS-like symptoms in a Wuhan hospital. Other sources point to December 8, 2019, as the date for the first undiagnosed appearance of a coronavirus infection.

Be that as it may, Chinese authorities only informed the WHO on December 31, 2019, about some cases of "pneumonia" in Wuhan, Hubei province. The WHO dutifully issued a communique on January 4, 2020. Accordingly, "China has reported to WHO a cluster of #pneumonia cases - with no deaths - in Wuhan, Hubei Province. Investigations are underway to identify the cause of this illness." Finally, on January 7, 2020, the Chinese authorities came clean and identified the disease as a new type of coronavirus. Yet, the central government did not impose a lockdown in Wuhan until January 23, 2020, and later gradually in other cities of Hubei province and beyond. Moreover, according to a just released CIA report, titled "U.N. - China: WHO Mindful But Not Beholden To China," and first reported by Newsweek, accused China of threatening to cut ties with WHO's coronavirus investigation team if the agency declared a global health emergency. Finally, on May 13, 2020, the CIA and the Department of Homeland Security (DHS) jointly accused China of targeting organizations in the United States of America that conduct coronavirus research with cyberattacks.

On the surface, the global system functioned as intended. However, at its core the system has given rise to a global health and economic catastrophe, because the Chinese information was based on a lie. The WHO and all the other countries that relied on its original communique initially were not informed participants but innocent bystanders in a farce, intentionally created by the President of the People's Republic of China, Xi Jinping, his colleagues in the Politburo, and their underlings throughout the country. While they were laughing up their sleeves, the rest of the world, including even those countries that benefited from Chinese largesses, have started to realize that they have become the victims of China's peculiar interpretation of friendship, solidarity, and "heavenly harmony" on earth.

In the meantime, governments across the globe have found themselves between the classic dilemma of the mythological Scylla and Charybdis, namely, attempting to balance saving human lives and keeping the economy functioning as close as possible to normal. Amidst this existential conundrum, the politicization of actions taken and emergency measures passed by every government in power could not come as a surprise. Is this condition of the world a healthy one? Certainly not. On the one hand, it is a lose-lose situation for every government and every politician to choose between two equally crucial life-and-death alternatives. On the other hand, decisions momentarily taken do not have the all powerful support of medical science, which, as of this writing, is still trying to find a vaccine against this novel coronavirus. Under these circumstances, decisions necessarily will be tainted with emotions on all sides of the political spectrum. In this light, decision making becomes octopus-like. It is almost impossible to escape its intellectually fraught ambiguity. For these reasons, the COVID-19 pandemic is a political, economic, financial, and cultural monster. The future will show its real lethality.

As of July 18, 2020, total confirmed world cases have exceeded 14.5 million, with the confirmed deaths having numbered over half a million, at 700,000. The United States of America alone has registered over 3.7 million confirmed cases. The death count is more than 140,000.. These numbers, however, are expected to change upward weekly.

As far as the United States of America is concerned, its cities are projected to lose $134 billion in 2020, $117 billion in 2021, and $110 billion in 2022, about $360 billion of total revenue through 2022, because of the economic damage caused by the pandemic. Most recently, Goldman Sachs Group Inc. has forecasted that the unemployment rate would peak at 25%, up from a previous forecast of 15%, as "more workers will lose their jobs and a larger share of them will be classified as unemployed." Their forecast has been based on the newest numbers, according to which, 13.3% of the American workforce have been unemployed as of June 9, 2020. Thus far, the total number of workers who have filed for jobless claims has reached 30 million.

While the loss of jobs has initially affected the hospitality industry, the pandemic induced jobless avalanche has spread to other areas of the national economy, including health care and other professional services. According to Federal Reserve chairman Jerome Powell: "Among people who were working in February, almost 40% of those in households making less than $40,000 a year had lost a job in March. This reversal of economic fortune has caused a level of pain that is hard to capture in words, as lives are up-ended amid great uncertainty about the future."

From a political perspective, Powell's last sentence is alarming. Clearly, lower income Americans have been bearing the lion's share of the COVID-19 pandemic's economic and financial consequences. Coupled with the steady decline of the prestige of all three branches of the government in America, the level of increased dissatisfaction with the work of the elected representatives and the unelected bureaucrats will definitely rise. The hate-mongering and intensely anti-American ultrarevolutionary politicians and the like-minded social movements will surely attack everyone who does not share their destructive views and everything that they consider to be detrimental to their extremist ideas. Ironically, their charges that the free market economy stifles freedom and equality, i.e. social justice, and practically enslaves, despoils, and impoverishes all minorities, point exactly to the catastrophic results of their radical agendas. If the economic and financial consequences of the COVID-19 pandemic are not remedied fairly quickly, this scurrilous and fringe opposition could grow in political influence, and seriously jeopardize the already fragile constitutional order of the United States of America.

Europe's largest economy, Germany's economy, shrank dramatically.

The GDP contracted in the first three months of 2020, by 2.2% compared to the previous quarter. Commensurately, household consumption fell sharply too. Investment in machinery and equipment plummeted. Exports and imports "saw a strong decline." France and Italy joined the German recession with even worse GDP numbers. In France GDP numbers declined by 5.8% in the first quarter of 2020. In Italy the same number was 4.7% in the first three months of 2020. In comparison, China's economy shrank in the first quarter of 2020, by 6.8% and not projected to grow by more than 1.2% throughout 2020.

The oil-rich Gulf monarchies have also experienced ballooning deficits. All six Gulf Cooperation Council (GCC) members, which includes Bahrain, Kuwait, Qatar, Saudi Arabia, and the United Arab Emirates, are searching for new sources of revenue. In addition, they have pledged to substantially reduce the ratio of foreign workers in their economies. A large number of those workers are Arabic-speaking from Egypt, Jordan, Syria, and Lebanon, and work in education, medicine, commerce, and the government. Indians, Bangladeshis, and Philippinos from Southeast Asia are also vital parts of the GCC economy. Combined, they have sent hundreds of millions of dollars back to their home countries, providing their extended families with the basic necessities of survival.

The COVID-19 pandemic has virtually brought the rest of the world economically and financially to its knees. As of the end of May, the confirmed coronavirus death toll in Africa officially stood at around 4,000. However, this number greatly underestimates the number of fatalities in the continent. Among those who succumbed to the coronavirus are the former President of the Republic of Congo Jacques Joachim Yhombi-Opango and Somalia's former Prime Minister Nur Hassan Hussein.

In South America, the hardest hit state by the coronavirus has been Brazil where the number of confirmed cases officially has surpassed 500,000. A total of 32,000 people died from the novel coronavirus. In addition, the pandemic has spread to every state of the Central and Southern Hemisphere. Presently, South America is considered the epicenter of the pandemic.

The hospitality, aviation, tourism, information technology, media, research and development, food, oil and gas, financial, banking, investment, import-export, shipping, agriculture, manufacturing sectors and industries have been ravaged by the ubiquitous lockdowns across the globe.

The socio-economic implications of the COVID-19 pandemic have been equally onerous. Social distancing, self-or-forced isolation, and travel restrictions have paralyzed entire cities, countries, regions, and continents, leading to the bankruptcy of many companies and the loss of millions of jobs. Schools have closed down too. The mostly unprepared health systems throughout the world have been overburdened, or have collapsed. Panic induced efforts to "flatten the curve" have only sparked heightened fear of an impending collapse of the political, financial, economic, and cultural realms of every state.

However, the price already paid for the lockdown and social distancing measures might be the highest within the individual families. Often, the most vulnarable members of the isolated families are the least aware of the calamity that they are participating actors in on a daily basis. In particular, children who are unconscious of their not so normal situation and thus understand very little, or nothing, could become victims in the center of individual and societal tragedies. With fears of a second wave of the CODOV-19 pandemic, times like these call for a comprehensive renewal strategy that must include measures of reintegration of the most vulnerable members of societies. Children cannot be allowed to fall through the cracks. Moreover, allowing the dictatorial takeover of the entire educational system by nefarious ideologues whose only agenda is to revolutionize the next generations on behalf of a utopian dictatorial government and against individual freedom will predictably only lead to a national catastrophe as well as the destruction of the greatest nation on earth.

Immediate, medium, and long term planning is required to avoid the proverbial vicious circle of bureaucratized public education. Governments must resist the political pressure of well organized teachers' unions across the globe. Home teaching, private school education, public-private elementary and high schools must be allowed to function as co-equals to the public education system. The opportunity to return to genuine teaching instead of indoctrination must be seized by the legislative and the executive branches throughout the world. Such a broad educational reform must be implemented if governments and societies do not want to risk an inexorable descent into a bottomless catastrophe. For children, teenagers, and adult students will never learn the fundamentals of democracy unless they are taught reality instead of lies and deceptions.

Another Roman wisdom says: "Quod nocet, saepe docet." What harms, often teaches. The time has come to expel the contradictions and lies that are inherent without exceptions in the political cultures and educations of every state in the world. For that to be accomplished, elected as well as non elected officials must seize the constitutional instruments of their individual and collective responsibilities for the good of their people. Only this way could peace and stability be achieved across the globe.

IV. The European Conundrum

As of the end of May 2020, the known cases of COVID-19 within the European Union have reached 2 million. The four member states that have reported the most cases are the United Kingdom (277,985), Spain (239,932), Italy (233,515), and Germany (182,370). The total number of deaths has reached 180,000. Lockdowns have been instituted in 26 of the 27 member states. The sole outlier has been Sweden that opted for the so-called "herd immunity."

Yet, even before the pandemic arrived on the continent, Europe in general and the European Union in particular have been subjected to multiple challenges. The breakup of the Soviet Union resulted first in the unification of the politically divided Germany and then in the wholesale admission of the majority of the Central and Eastern European states into the European Union. Meanwhile, the new Russian Federation has oscillated between moving closer to the European Union as well as the United States of America and simultaneously trying to rebuild a politically truncated state. The financial crisis that began in 2007 and lasted until 2012, caused on the average a 4% shrinkage in the economies of the member states and an average of 5% potential loss in manufacturing output throughout the European Union. Until the COVID 19 pandemic, this financial and economic crisis was the deepest recession since the 1930. Albeit the sovereign debt crisis was unexpected and the various organs of the European Union were inadequately prepared for it, a financial catastrophe was avoided, because of the compensatory fiscal policy responses of the European Central Bank (ECB) and the corrective actions of the national banks of the member states. However, on the whole, the post crisis recovery has not been well thought out and has been insufficiently implemented. Potential output has not been raised evenly, the flexibility of labor markets has not been improved adequately, fiscal consolidation has been lagging behind the required minimum, intra-European Union adjustments have not been carried out efficiently, and global imbalances have not been eliminated.

Adding insult to injury, the initial responses of Brussels and the individual member states to the appearance of the new coronavirus on the continent have been half-hearted and weak, because of the European Union's increasingly growing dependence on China trade and investments. In addition to the burgeoning public health crisis within the member states and beyond, the various organizations of the European Union should have dealt with the latent shortfalls in public and private investments. Following the US Federal Reserve's lead, the European Central Bank has abandoned its rules for limiting sovereign and corporate bank purchases and has embarked on a 750 billion Euro ($811 billion) Pandemic Emergency Purchase Program in early March 2020. In conjunction with the program, the majority of the member states have initiated stimulus measures to support their economies. The central program and the states' measures combined have provided companies with some liquidity to avoid an avalanche of bankruptcies and maintain a sufficient level of productive capacity. Moreover, additional financial rescue packages have been offered to the particularly hard hit sectors of the economies. Finally, cash monies have been disbursed quickly to individuals households, in order to prevent negative political repercussions from the sudden loss of regular incomes.

In spite of these short term measures, every national economy within the European Union has experienced a nosedive. Particularly hard hit have been the economies of the Central and Eastern European states, which historically have been always lagging behind their West European allies. In addition, the hard hit states of Southern Europe by the pandemic, Italy, France, and Spain, have experienced a noticeable drop in standard of living too. As a result, for the first time since the breakup of the Soviet Union, poverty has been rising in several of the member states. Ideas to prevent further damage to the economies of the member states abound.

Apparently the most favored has been the one outlined by the German Council of Economic Experts under the title "European Redemption Fund." Pursuant to this concept, member states would be able to transfer portions of their public debts exceeding 60%-of-GDP limits set by EU rules to a common refinancing platform. Simultaneously, the states would obligate themselves to join repayment plans, through which they would cover their thus transferred debts over the timespan of 20 to 25 years.

On May 18, 2020, German Chancellor Angela Merkel and French President Emmanuel Macron have agreed on establishing a joint European

Recovery Fund amounting to 500 billion Euros ($543 billion). According to their joint announcement, the Fund will provide grants to regions and economic sectors most affected by the COVID-19 pandemic. The money will be allocated for a specialized recovery fund within the next seven year program regulating annual European Union budgets. Their joint statement, simultaneously released in Berlin and Paris states that the Fund "will be used in a targeted manner to meet the challenges of the pandemic and its aftermath." At the joint press conference, the French President declared that the money will be released as a grant and not as a loan to the recipients. However, the German Chancellor clarified that the grant will have to be reimbursed "through several future European budgets." It appears that this joint German-French initiative has met with the instant approval of Ursula von der Leyen, head of the European Union Commission, who opined that the initiative "rightly puts the emphasis on the need to work on a solution with the European budget at its core."

If adopted unanimously by the European Union Council, a major source of disagreement between the member states regarding the issuance of joint Eurobonds versus the current German-French initiative could be resolved amicably. It must be noted here that the talks on the 2021-2027 Multiannual Financial Framework (MFF) stalled in February, because the more affluent member states objected to sharing the debt with the other member states most affected by the pandemic. While the initiative will double the solidarity fund, the European Union's Economic Commissioner let it be known that, contrary to Ursula von der Leyen's assertion, the thus created 1 trillion Euros Fund ($1.1 trillion) will not be sufficient. He claims that the European Union would need 1.5 trillion Euros to prevent the single market from being "broken in two."

The German-French initiative also ran into opposition from the Netherlands, Austria, Denmark, and Sweden. Speaking on behalf of these four member states, the Dutch Prime Minister Mark Rutte let it be known that he and his colleagues are working on an alternative proposal. Without elaborating on the details of their proposal, Prime Minister Rutte said that they would like to add tougher conditions for the loans. For good measure he also said the following: "There will be a lot of proposals." Most likely he referred to the European Union's Executive Commission that already signaled its intention to submit in the near future its own proposal.

This proposal has been made public on May 17, 2020. Accordingly, the Commission has proposed borrowing $8.49 billion on the financial markets to spend on vaccines, drugs, and healthcare over the next 4 years. This proposal, also must be approved by all 27 member states. It would be added to the $2.6 billion emergency fund, which could be available to cover medical shortages within the Union, highlighted by the COVID-19 pandemic. Echoing President Trump, the announcement states: "Europe should strive to strengthen its strategic autonomy by reducing excessive import dependence for the most-needed goods and services, such as medical products and pharmaceuticals."

As recently as on April 20, 2020, George Soros also chimed in by proposing the sale of "perpetual bonds," on which the principal does not have to be repaid (although they can be repurchased or redeemed at the issuer's discretion). He justified his idea by saying that the European Union is facing a once-in-a-lifetime war against a deadly virus that is threatening not only people's lives, but also the very survival of the Union. Soros' argument is grievously weakened by his conclusion, according to which the solution for a unified Europe is open borders, his global visionary ultima ratio.

Beyond the rich-and-poor divide that has plagued the European Union from its inception, the anomalous cacophony of political voices incessantly pulling the member states away from steadily burgeoning unity toward even more definite dissensions. Legally as well as morally, the European Union has been founded on a collection of "European values" that rest, according to Article 2 of the Treaty of the European Union, "on the values of respect for human dignity, freedom, democracy, equality, the rule of law and respect for human rights, including the rights of persons belonging to minorities. These values are common to the Member States in a society in which pluralism, non-discrimination, tolerance, justice, solidarity and equality between women and man prevail."

These are noble and laudable, although clearly maximalist aspirations within an incomplete, imperfect, and historically divergent economic and political union of 27 member states. On the positive side of the ledger, the European Union and its predecessor the European Economic Community have secured almost seven decades of peace and increasing prosperity for the continent. In 1995, the Schengen Agreement abolished almost all of the European Union's internal borders, enabling passport-free movement across most of the Union. On January 1, 1999, the European Monetary Union was created, with a single currency, the Euro, which has already replaced the local currencies in 19 member states.

Oppositely, the European Union has been dying of a political disease that has manifested itself from its inception; the unconquerable disorder of internal crises within several of the member states. Undoubtedly, this disorder has been fueled by a multitude of local nationalistic, ethnic, religious, cultural, and linguistic differences and even fanaticism. The accumulated results of all these differences and fanaticism are the universal political crises which have torn Europe apart from times immemorial. From the French Revolution at the end of the 18th century, through the Napoleonic Wars and the horrors of the first half of the 20th century, the entire continent has been convulsed by two irreconcilable ideologies. In the West, throughout two centuries, gradual progress has been achieved toward full-fledged democracy. In the East, a region saturated historically with despotic traditions, states have found themselves in all sorts of difficulties following the collapse of the Soviet Union.

In reality, the challenge to democratic values has always been a political war between two irreconcilable ideologies. In the West, relatively well organized republics exist. In the East, mainly in the so-called Visegrad Four, so named after a small town in Hungary, and consisting of Poland, Hungary, the Czech Republic and Slovakia, opposition against the majorities in Brussels, Strasbourg, and The Hague, have been growing steadily. Resistance and Euroscepticism are the ideologies de jour, which already have taken roots also in the political lives of Romania and Bulgaria, as well as across the Balkan states and beyond.

Especially, since the migrant crisis of 2015, many member states have been in open revolt against what they perceived as Brussels' hostile dictates against their national interests. Indeed, different historical experiences have already weighed heavily on the East-West divide as early as 2004. Member states that belonged for over four decades to the "Soviet bloc" have resented the leading role of Germany, equating it with the political tyranny of the former Soviet Union, while viewing the faceless army of bureaucrats in Brussels as the Western reincarnation of the dogmatic apparatchiks in the

Kremlin. This situation has been exacerbated further by the fact that neither the Western block nor the Eastern group of member states appeared to demonstrate any principled coherence. In brief, the decision making within the Union has become unpredictable and measures thus concluded have mostly been the result of unprincipled compromises. The emblematic example of this behavior has been Poland, which has oscillated between being a "troublemaker" by blocking the Intergovernmental Conference (IGC) of 2004, while in foreign policy and national security matters has shown itself a super-enthusiastic European member state.

A more serious problem for the European Union has been presented by Hungary, because of the authoritarian inclinations of and the propensity for radical actions by its Prime Minister, Viktor Orban. Having regained power in 2010, with a two thirds majority in the unicameral Parliament (Orszaghaz), he commenced to transform Hungary behind the veil of democracy into a one-party autocracy. Branded by the European Parliament as a "systematic threat to the rule of law" and functioning under the threat of Article 7 procedure of the Treaty on the European Union, the Orban-led government has reestablished the pre-World War II model of Miklos Horthy's semi-fascist Hungary, sprinkled with a large dose of Soviet-style despotism. Calling all this "illiberal democracy," he has proceeded to adapt the political playbook of Presidents Putin and Erdogan. Fittingly, he has eliminated any formal and informal opposition to his rule and has taken possession of the Hungarian economy. Moreover, in 2014 and in 2018, during the last two general elections, he used numerous fraudulent schemes to maintain his party's two thirds majority in the Parliament, while not gaining even 50% of the votes cast. General corruption has skyrocketed. Money laundering has become the norm for Viktor Orban and his small coterie of friends. The little remaining money has been spent liberally on promoting his favorite pastime, European football. After having lost big in the midterm elections in the fall, he has used his emergency powers under the COVID-19 pandemic, with unparalleled scope within the European Union, to suffocate financially the capital city of Budapest and any other city, county, district, and village that dared to vote against his Party, the acronym of which in Hungarian ironically is FIDESZ, meaning the Alliance of Young Democrats. Recently, Hungary again allied itself with Beijing and declared its firm opposition to the admission of Taiwan to the WHO.

Yet, the most impactful action of the Eurosceptics occurred in the United Kingdom where a referendum in 2016, in which 52% voted to leave and 48% voted to remain in the European Union, resulted in the withdrawal agreement on January 31, 2020. Dubbed the Brexit, a portmanteau of "British" and "exit," the United Kingdom's decoupling from the European Union has established a dangerous precedent for future separations from an organization whose main objective has been to unify the entire continent under a single government. More significantly, the political process by which the decoupling happened were fraught with vicious infightings that resulted in the resignations of two Prime Ministers, the Conservatives David Cameron and Theresa May. It is not too difficult to predict that the issues raised by the Brexit debate will linger for the political future of the United Kingdom. Regardless of the internal upheavals that surrounded Brexit, the early general election on December 12, 2019, resulted in a decisive victory for the Conservatives against the Labor Party. The question of how closely the United Kingdom would be tied to the European Union will remain the subject of future negotiations. However, the longer these negotiations would drag on, the more likely that they would further aggravate the existing and thus far unknown future disagreements among the remaining member states.

Fundamentally, however, the principal disagreement among the remaining 27 member states centers around what they call "base values." Of course, the meaning of these values, as essentially defined in Article 2 of the Treaty as liberal and democratic, lends itself to a variety of interpretations. Yet, beyond the infighting over interpretations, the more pressing issue remains whether the member states can agree on the basic principles of the extent of collective limitations on their national sovereignty. In the absence of such an agreement, the European Union will continue to present a chaotic assembly of unruly states, especially in the fields of foreign and national security policies.

This chaotic state of affairs has been on display on a daily basis within and outside the European Union. Grandiloquently termed as "European values" rooted in the history of the continent since the Enlightenment, such as respect for human dignity and human rights, fundamental freedoms, equality of citizens before the law, the rule of law, and parliamentary democracy, these values have been threatened continuously by the frequent overreach and even illegal intrusions of unelected European Union bureaucrats into the domestic domains of the member states.

Actions always draw reactions. Presently, in the wake of Brexit and the financial and economic hardships caused by the pandemic, the European Union is experiencing multiple challenges to its declared "base values." Although Brussels has tried to downplay the seriousness of the political forces that are highly critical of the fundamentals of the European Union, these centripetal movements are gathering strength, and winning elections in both local and national levels. In this respect, Viktor Orban's "illiberal democracy" has been since 2015 the proverbial canary in a coal mine. Thus far, all the major institutions of the European Union have treated Hungary with kid gloves. Clearly it has been a mistake. Viktor Orban's corruption of the European Union's value system is fatal for the future progress of the organization. In practice, his "illiberal democracy" is the copycat of Erdogan's and Putin's hard authoritarianism. For these reasons, if his sick idea about democracy will be allowed to further metastasize, Viktor Orban's authoritarianism could mean the end of the European Union as the world knows it.

Moreover, as could have been expected, the relativization of the member states' sovereignty in foreign affairs has become a major source of disagreements within the European Union. Consequently, the European Union's foreign policy is a chaotic mess. Pompously called the High Representative of the Union for Foreign Affairs and Security Policy, the occupant has been the chief coordinator of the Common Foreign and Security Policy of the European Union. This position is presently held by the Spaniard Josep Borrell Fontelles who is mainly limited to randomly conceived declarations about a variety of topics that have been ignored regularly by the member states. For example, mandated to set foreign policy by consensus, Mr. Borrell released his third statement sharply condemning Israel under his own name. Supported by 25 out of the 27 member states, Borrell declared: "We strongly urge Israel to refrain from any unilateral decision that would lead to the annexation of any occupied territory and would be as such contrary to international law."

Putting aside the fact that Mr. Borrell's statement is erroneous in several aspects, the Foreign Minister of Austria Alexander Schallenberg rejected Borrell's "prejudice" against Israel and called to invite the Foreign Minister of Israel Gabi Ashkenazi to a European Union Foreign Affairs Council's meeting. The Foreign Minister of Hungary Peter Szijjarto joined his Austrian colleague in dissent. However, the Hungarian Foreign Minister ran into trouble with his Israeli counterpart Gabi Ashkenazi, when he claimed incorrectly that the two discussed and agreed on identity politics, sovereignty, national security, and their joint opposition against illegal immigration in the European context too. In his official rebuttal, the Israeli Foreign Minister immediately reacted to his Hungarian colleague's assertion and stated that the two never discussed the topics brought up by Mr. Szijjarto. Regrettably, such a rogue diplomatic initiative has been the rule and not the exception within the European Union. In meekly worded utterances bureaucrats in Brussels opined that Mr. Borrell, as Mr. Szijjarto, might have expressed his own opinion. What the unelected bureaucrats in Brussels forgot to mention as a motive for Mr. Borrell's action is the existence of disproportionately high and irresponsibly extended investments that the European Union has undertaken on behalf of an improbable future Palestinian state.

To round up the circle of foreign policy follies by the European Union, Mr. Borrell was also accused of watering down a disinformation report that was highly critical of China, which he vehemently denied. Yet, in spite of his denial, European Union politicians told foreign diplomats that Mr. Borrell and his people were "caught with their hand in the cookie jar." Be that as it may, the first version of the European Union's report contained the statement "global disinformation campaign" by the People's Republic of China, words that did not appear in the second and final version of the report.

Citizens across the European Union must be furious with Brussels and Mr. Borrell for a more substantial reason too. The European Union's bureaucrats have for some time been conducting a campaign for the People's Republic of China and against the United States of America. In that respect, a fundamental question arises: Do the bureaucrats in Brussels really imagine that Beijing could replace the United States of America as a global ally for the European Union? The relative international importance of the European Union and its integrity as a global player rest upon its political, military, and economic alliance with the United States of America. NATO is a principal military alliance upon which the stability and peace of Europe and the rest of the world are founded.

Outdoing himself in superhuman arrogance and idiocy, Mr. Borrell sounded the alarm about Europe's "existential crisis," allegedly sparked by the COVID-19 pandemic. Studiously avoiding calling it the "Chinese" or "Wuhan" virus, Mr. Borrell launched into a global policy lecture at a virtual German Ambassadors' Conference 2020. His rambling presentation was opened with the claim that pressure to choose sides between the United States of America and the People's Republic of China is growing amidst the arrival of an "Asian century." Warming to his ideologically loaded topic, Mr. Borrell opined that the pandemic could be considered a "great accelerator of history." In the same vein, he asserted that the People's Republic is quickly becoming "more powerful and assertive." Arriving at the crescendo of his speech, Mr. Borrell made the following statement: "Analysts have long talked about the end of an American-led system and the arrival of an Asian century. This is now happening in front of our eyes. If the 21st century turns out to be an Asian century, as the 20th was an American one, the pandemic may well be remembered as the turning point of this process."

Clearly, Mr. Borrell cannot comprehend the not so negligible fact that by echoing the prevailing European mentality, he revealed the continent's uncertain state of mind about the world's reality. The European Union that prides itself on representing "the European values," essentially European civilization, cannot use its despair over its internal failures to justify its own destruction. The organization that desires to unite the entire continent must not prostrate itself before an aggressively expanding despotic regime, in order to save itself. Finally, it is impossible for a civilization to preserve and expand its basic values of freedom, democracy, and respect for the rule of law by bowing to the Chinese Communist Party's dictates, when the leaders of the European Union do not realize how powerfully President Xi and his colleagues work to destroy everything that Europe represents. Instead of promulgating idiotic ideas, Mr. Borrell should elaborate on how to defend European principles, which are and will remain the foundation of the continent's stable, prosperous, and peaceful future.

Accordingly, Mr. Borrell should adhere to the reality that the political system of the People's Republic of China is a classic despotism, in which a single state party monopolizes all the powers and exerts absolute control over all the organs of the government, down to the tiniest locality. In addition to the irreconcilable political differences, the European and the

Chinese cultures are as opposite to one another as a polar bear to a camel. To anticipate that economic growth and prosperity would lead to a less despotic form of government in the People's Republic of China is nothing but an intellectual exercise in futility. In its external relations, Beijing would never be satisfied with reciprocal political, economic, and legal equality. By its very nature, the Chinese Communist Party is a control freak. For these reasons, its leaders do not strive for cooperation but attempt to achieve at any cost subordination. If nothing else, the history of Tibet's subjugation and the current example of Hong Kong's tragedy should be unambiguous warnings for the European Union and the rest of the world.

More significantly, German Chancellor Angela Merkel said in a video speech to the Konrad-Adenauer-Stiftung in Berlin on May 27, 2020, that the European Union has a "great strategic interest" in maintaining cooperation with the People's Republic of China. In spite of the numerous grievances that the European Union has with Beijing, she rated the relationship as a "top priority" when Germany will take over a rotating presidency on July 1. In her speech, she elaborated further: "We Europeans will need to recognize the decisiveness with which China will claim a leading position in the existing structures of the international architecture." She closed her speech by assuring her listeners that she will aim at maintaining a "critical, constructive" dialog with Beijing.

Brussels' strategy for Asia is also rich in high flying ideas but fairly meager in their implementation. Defining the European Union's strategy as "sustainable, comprehensive and rules-based connectivity," which will "contribute to the enhanced prosperity, safety and resilience of people and societies in Europe and Asia," cannot possibly be taken seriously. In addition to being woefully China-centric, this so-called strategy places the European Union way behind the other major players on the continent. To be less merciful, the European Union is not a serious factor in Asia at all.

The European Union's and Africa's relations are governed by the Cotonou Agreement and the Joint Africa-EU Strategy. The first covers a total of 79 states across Africa, the Caribbean, and the Pacific region. The Agreement's main focus is on eradicating poverty and promoting gradual integration of these states into the world economy. To achieve these laudable goals, the Agreement emphasizes three areas: development cooperation, economic and trade cooperation, and political aspects. The Joint Africa-EU Strategy has a narrower reach. Adopted in 2007, it relies on periodic action plans that were laid out in a roadmap on April 2-3, 2014. Its focus is on "peace and security," "democracy and good governance, including human rights," "human development," "sustainable and inclusive development and growth and continental integration," and "global and emerging issues." Again, elevated rhetoric and precious little tangible plans for actual implementations.

Behind the pompous language and exaggerated global intentions, the European Union resembles the proverbial monkey who wants to grab all the visible bananas without having the means for it, namely, the absolutely necessary two hands and arms, in which those bananas could be collected. Inert within the European Union and mostly insignificant across the globe, Mr. Borrell's office hovers between the chaotic and the insignificant. Clearly, the international achievements of the European Union bear the stamp of these shortcomings. Pressed between the reality of fatal weakness and the collective desire to be significant, the European Union is suspended between two realities, its dependence on the United States of America for protection and its dislike of the status quo. Meanwhile, the joint European military force is still a pipedream. This ambiguity will continue to linger and with it the fatal weakness of the European Union will remain excruciatingly permanent. Deplorably, the future will demonstrate the European Union's fundamental lack of enduring viability.

Essentially, the existence of the future of the Western alliance is at stake. When the pandemic is finally over and life will return to normal, bilateral, regional, and global issues must be clarified. The crisis that was created by the French Revolution and by the Napoleanic conquests destroyed the Holy Roman Empire. The subsequent decision by the Habsburgs to abandon their western territories and to compensate themselves for the losses in the east ultimately led to the demise of the empire one century later. The European Union is at a crossroads. Triggered by its many shortcomings and exacerbated by the Chinese COVID-19 pandemic, the edifice of the grandiose vision of European unity is about to crumble. The 27 member states of the European Union must make an unequivocal decision. This decision cannot come soon enough. It must be a no-brainer for the heads of the member states. The People's Republic of China would cause the destruction of the entire continent's future. Strengthening the alliance with the United States of America is the only right decision that they can make. If they fail to act, they will take a better future away from their people and will condemn future generations to utter misery.

Meanwhile, after having argued about the content of the recovery package for six months, leaders of the European Union reached agreement about a landmark €1.82 trillion budget. European council President Charles Michel called the seven-year budget and recovery package a "good deal." European Commission President Ursula von der Leyen was less happy with the outcome and bemoaned the concessions made to cut "modern policies" in research and innovation. Emanuel Macron called the deal an "historic day for Europe."

At the center of the agreement is €750 billion in grants and loans to counter the impact of the pandemic within the European Union. Disbursement of funds shall be linked to governments respecting the rule of law. Hungary and Poland threatened to veto the agreement if it adopted a policy of withholding funds from nations who do not meet certain democratic principles.

The European Parliament must approve this deal. If the linkage between the availability of funds and the democratic values is not taken seriously, the so-called democratic deficit of the European Union in general and the illiberal tendencies in Eastern Europe will make a mockery out of the principles of democracy throughout the European Union. The danger is that some member states will pay lip service to the European values to obtain the monies they need, and then continue violating basic legal principles to the detriment of their citizens.

Only time will tell whether this agreement is proof of more integration or simply the continuation of business as usual, in which the formerly communist dictatorships would game the system for their economic and political advantage.

V. The Media That Cried Wolf One
Time Too Many

The Boy Who Cried Wolf is one of Aesop's widely known Fables. In it, the main character, a boy, repeatedly fools the villagers into thinking that a wolf is attacking their herd of goats. When finally a wolf appears and the boy sounds the alarm again the villagers ignore the boy's call, believing it to be false. As a result, the goats are eaten by the wolf. The moral of the fable in the Greek version is: "This shows how liars are rewarded. Even if they tell the truth, no one believes them." In an alternative but not contradictory perspective, the lonely boy who is out in the wilderness for weeks, or even months, craves human companionship and attention. The only way to break his loneliness is to invent something that surely will bring a great deal of instant empathy for himself. While the boy's actions are highly irresponsible, in spite of his gnawing loneliness, the villagers are the real victims of his false claims. Individual misery collides with collective fear. More generally, dishonesty attracts ubiquitous rejection.

Once again, the American media coverage of the COVID-19 pandemic has demonstrated the utter professional incompetence and ideologically tainted irresponsibility of the self-indulgent "fourth estate." Like the lonely shepherd boy in Aesop's fable, members of the written and electronic media have been hell-bent to absolutely control the narrative, regardless of its veracity. Having claimed initially that the seasonal flu is more dangerous than the novel coronavirus, the media, with scant exceptions, have quickly moved into overdrive to describe the destructive toll of the new disease on humans and the alleged incompetence of the President as well as the federal government. As could have been expected in the era of Trump, the coup de grace has been the extreme and overwhelmingly one-sided politicization of the pandemic by the media. While the pandemic has seriously damaged the economy and unemployment skyrocketed, the bulk of the so-called journalists have ignored the decidedly positive measures taken by the White House as well as the entire Executive Branch, because they have been busy pursuing their own nefarious political agendas.

On the other hand, the daily briefings on the COVID-19 situation by New York governor Andrew Cuomo, have been reported by both the written and electronic media without any negative comments. On the contrary, his love fest with his younger brother Chris on CNN has been hailed as perfection itself. Voices demanded that the Democrat Party replace its presumptive nominee Joe Biden with Andrew Cuomo have multiplied with every passing day. The fact that he provided immunity against prosecution to the managers of elderly care facilities and the deadly effects of his decree, in which he ordered infected patients to be sent back to those facilities from the hospitals, were never brought up by the media. Neither has ever mentioned that President Trump and his task force have provided the state with all the federal assistance that has been requested promptly.

Whether by accident or by design, it has been a fact since the so-called October or Red Revolution in 1917, that two strongly discernable tendencies have characterized the editorial policies of two influential East Coast dailies, The New York Times and the Washington Post. Firstly, to keep the bulk of the American people as near to news dependency on these two newspapers as appeared consistent with minimal factual information about domestic and international affairs. Secondly, to preserve the vast majority of the nation as close to the verge of political illiteracy by means of irresponsible ignorance and outright lies as was compatible with the continuation of maintaining these two newspapers' monopoly over the flow of information within and outside the United States of America.

Regardless, one cannot escape the conclusion that the editors of these two newspapers have been tenaciously pursuing a course of which the object has been to promote anti-constitutional and anti-American programs. Their means included every conceivable act, whatever their ethical character, or political consequences, which hold promise to facilitate the attainment of their end, namely, the overthrow of the Republic and its replacement with an economically egalitarian Socialism and even utopian Communism in the United States of America. Although Mark Twain claimed that "No amount of evidence will ever persuade an idiot," holding the view that the American people are all stupid speak for these newspapers' arrogance, contempt, and condescension for their actual or potential readers.

To illustrate the validity of the intellectual dishonesty and the moral corruption of these two newspapers from the past, it is sufficient to bring up the name of Walter Duranty. Having been adorned with the prestigious Pulitzer Prize for a series of reports about the Soviet Union, published mostly throughout 1931, and deified as an ultimate source of wisdom on the early years of Stalin's reign, this Moscow Bureau Chief of the New York Times for 14 years (1922-1936) denied the widespread famine of 1932-1933. To make matters worse, he kept mum about the beginning of the purges, depicted Stalin as a saint who devoted his life 24/7 for the betterment of the Soviet Union and the lives of its inhabitants, and pictured life in the Soviet Union as a wonderful existence in an earthly paradise.

In the height of the Great Depression, on February 4, 1931, Duranty enthusiastically wrote about "the greatest wave of immigration in modern history." Referring to the gullible and desperate unemployed in the United States of America who undertook the journey into the unknown, he prophesied: "When the day comes that foreign workers here (the Soviet Union) may write home and say, 'Things are pretty good here, why don't you come along? There are jobs for everybody and plenty to eat. Russia is not so bad a place in which to live and there are no lay-offs or short time and you get all that is coming to you.'....Then immigration to the Soviet Union will begin to rival the flood that poured into America. At the present rate of progress that day is not far distant." To corroborate Duranty's glowing reportage about the "workers' paradise," in which an abyss divided conditions in the United States of America and the Soviet Union, The New York Times printed in full on October 11, 1931, a lecture given on American national radio by George Bernard Shaw. This blubber head in chief of his era stated: "Well my first impression was that Russia is full of Americans. My second was that every intelligent Russian has been in America and didn't like it because he had no freedom there." Moreover, to reinforce his reputation as an incorrigible idiot, he added: "...proletarians of all hands are welcome if they can pull their weight in the Russian boat...There is hope everywhere in Russia because these evils are retreating there before the spread of Communism as steadily as they are advancing upon us before the last desperate struggle of our bankrupt Capitalism to stave off its inevitable doom. You will not go to Russia to smell out the evils you can see without leaving your own doorstep." Yet, when the poor souls that believed in those lies spread so irresponsibly by The New York Times perished in Stalin's Gulag as American spies, the newspaper remained deafeningly silent.

Following the disintegration of the Soviet Union, when the old archives were opened, the truth came out about Stalin's reign. The New York Times, which submitted his articles for the Pulitzer Prize in 1932, wrote in 1990, that Duranty's work was "some of the worst reporting to appear in this newspaper." Question: Where were the editors of The New York Times in the 1920s and 1930s, and after 1953, when Nikita Khrushchev revealed the blood curdling details of Stalin's terror? The founding fathers gave a free Republic to the American people, provided they "can keep it." Abuse of the freedoms granted in the constitution, including freedom of the press, cannot be corrupted intentionally without causing lasting damage to the entire democratic fabric of government.

The undignified and self-abasing behavior of The New York Times has continued unabated throughout the 20th and the first two decades of the 21st centuries. Clearly, at The New York Times history has always repeated itself in the worst possible ways. Joined by The Washington Post, these two newspapers have become the written media mouthpieces of all the anti-democratic forces, in which all the crazy and distorted ideas of the political Left have been published first and have influenced the political discourse most powerfully. Moreover, on the editorial and commentary pages of these two newspapers the two spectrums of American politics, the conservative and the liberal, have collided: the urbanized elitists with the inhabitants of the countrysides, the African Americans with the mostly white people, the new immigrants with everybody else, the entire population with the local, state, and federal governments, and the villages with the townships and the larger cities.

While the pandemic has been still in flux, The New York Times in an opinion piece on May 10, 2020, accused President Trump of wanting to start "a new cold war to deflect attention from his failures." Coauthored by Rachel Esplin Odell and Stephen Wertheim and titled "Can the Democrats Avoid Trump's China Trap," this opinion piece torturously attempted to develop the thesis that President Trump is determined to fight the coronavirus enemy with "verbal and physical firepower." Through this false assertion, the authors arrive at their even more outrageous conclusion: "...the Trump Administration appears to be setting its target on a foreign power: China, where the outbreak appears to have started but which is hardly responsible for the United States being the most infected country in the world." Uh Oh! That enduring ghost of Walter Duranty! Reading further, the authors reiterate their belief that no proof exists of the Chinese origin of COVID-19: "Now Secretary of State Mike Pompeo is declaring that there is "a significant amount of evidence" that the virus originated in a Chinese laboratory, though has provided no proof." This monstrous disinformation is followed by an utterly idiotic comparison: "The accusation, although doubted by scientists and intelligence agencies, may lead the public to blame China for the pandemic, much as the George W. Bush administration, through suggestion more than outright lies, convinced seven in 10 Americans in 2003 that Saddam Hussein of Iraq was likely involved in the Sept. 11 attacks." What "scientists?" What "intelligence agencies?" Then, following a dire warning about a cold war with "the world's No. 2 power," the authors stated that "Mr. Trump seeks to avoid responsibility for a pandemic that the White House was slower still to take seriously." The journalistic standards of The New York Times in their brazen misery.

Not to be outdone, The Washington Post also ran an opinion piece by Paul Waldman under the title "Yes, Donald Trump is to blame for this depression." Claiming that the President prefers saving the economy rather than human lives, the author declares giddily "In fact, this depression is absolutely Trump's fault. He made a series of disastrous decisions that led us to this point, and other countries that have had far different experiences illustrate what might have happened if we had a president who wasn't so utterly incompetent." After rumbling on in the same fashion, the author concluded thus: "Just look at other countries that have been more effective in combating the virus and dealing with the economic fallout. No one is unscathed, and there has been economic damage everywhere. But where the leaders acted quickly and made smart choices, the situation has been far better." Again, as the authors of the opinion piece in The New York Times, this author writes in generalities too. What "countries" and what "leaders?" What did they do better than the Trump Administration? Did they have more foresight? Did they mobilize immediately or early enough? In conclusion, the readers do not get objective and factual information. Instead, they are force-fed a biased opinion that is full of irrational hatred against President Trump, erroneous disinformation, and unfounded conclusions.

More generally, Van Gordon Sauter, former CBS News president opined, according to Fox News Network's media analyst Howard Kurtz, that the daily newspapers across the United States of America are decidedly liberal. For good measure, he included in his review the three major news television networks and two of the leading cable news outfits. Moreover, he claimed that this leftward tilt had been accelerated by their loathing of President Trump. Finally, he concluded that to many journalists objectivity, balance, and fairness are not mandatory in a divided political era and in a country they believe to be severely flawed.

Indeed, appearing to play music from the same sheet, the overwhelming majority of the electronic media have been blasting uniformly biased tunes in orchestrated unison. For more than three years, NBC, CNBC, MSNBC, ABC, and CBS have regaled their American and international viewers with the so-called Russia collusion. Providing unlimited access to former and current bureaucrats and so-called whistleblowers of questionable integrity, while denying equal access to anyone who did not fit their narratives, these organizations have made a mockery of objective reporting. Claiming that they all have had compelling evidence of criminal conspiracies between the Trump campaign and President Putin himself to rig the presidential election of 2016, all these television channels have disseminated daily lies in organized unison. When the bubble has burst, however, no explanations or mea culpas have been issued by them. Having been exposed as unmitigated fools with a perverted understanding of free speech and the notion of the freedom of the press, their moral sense of right and wrong has been tarnished forever. Finally, their cunning and deceit have only elicited contemptuous disrespect.

Recently, emerging from his basement sanctuary in Delaware, Joe Biden was interviewed by CNN's Dana Bash immediately after the Memorial Day holiday. As reported by FNC's Brian Flood and sarcastically described by NewsBusters managing editor Curtis Houck, "Naturally Trump-hating and fear-loving CNN served Tuesday as Joe Biden's first in-person interview since the coronavirus pandemic began and, right on cue, chief political correspondent Dana Bash fulfilled her role as a real-life Bashful, liberal foot soldier, and citizen of Zuckerville. Between softball questions and assisting Biden in touting anti-Trump conspiracy theories, it was mission accomplished." Continuing his description of the interview, he opined thus: "Of course, Bash refused to ask about Tara Reade or the refusal from the University of Delaware to release any of Biden's Senate papers that could provide the public more information on what was internally written at the time of Reade's allegations. So much for journalism." Instead, he noted, Bash focused on Trump "trying to belittle" Biden for wearing a mask in public.

Even Mediaite's Tommy Christopher, a dedicated liberal with an abiding hatred for President Trump, criticized in his Twitter bio Bash's interview. "The most infuriating, yet encouraging, parts of the interview were when Biden was not just asked extremely stupid questions, but was then pressed on those extremely stupid questions. The first of these was related to Trump's mockery of Biden for wearing a mask in public on Memorial Day… there are a lot of ways for a journalist to approach this issue." In conclusion, Christopher noted that Bash could have remarked that President Trump's comments contradicted his own experts, or simply asked for a response and let Biden go to the town. "But Bash went on with 'He is trying to belittle you for wearing a mask, making it seem like it's a sign of weakness. Is it?'" Finally, he exploded thus: "Now some people might defend this by saying these journalists are just asking the question, maybe acting as stand-ins for a significant portion of their audience, which is, after all, their jobs. I would argue that when a significant portion of the audience wonders something so stupid, it becomes the journalist's job to educate them, not play along. This is where the (extremely weak) audience surrogate excuse falls away, because Bash then asked Biden 'So do you think wearing the mask projects strength or weakness?'"

Demonstrating that truth in reporting does not seem to matter any more, CNN anchor Don Lemon accused President Trump in his May 17, 2020, nightly handoff with fellow anchor Chris Cuomo of "trafficking" in racial hatred that resulted in the police-caused death of George Floyd of Minneapolis, Minnesota. Mr. Lemon also suggested that President Trump by his actions have encouraged African-Americans to carry out more racially motivated violent deeds: "Imagine if that was me on the ground how you would feel as a friend, as someone I spend a lot of time with. Imagine how people around this country feel when their friends like you, both of us are a different background. When their friends say nothing. When they do nothing." Then he ranted on: "How many more excuses do you need to make before you examine yourself and say, 'OK, maybe I need to wake up a little bit and take a good, long look at what I've been doing." No longer addressing his anchor friend he continued: "Maybe I need to understand or realize that the environment that this President has trafficked in can help to lead to these sort of behavior, meaning the people who are doing these things - the people who are calling the cops on people falsely in Central Park, the people who are chasing people down the street in Georgia and killing them - that you may begin to think that your actions are normal. That you may begin to think that you as the preeminent voice can do things that are inhuman to other people and it will be accepted." This hysterical and idiotic diatribe is identity politics mingled with outright racial hatred. Pure and simple. Nothing about the murders in Chicago, New York City, Baltimore, Denver, Los Angeles, Washington, D.C., St, Louis, and elsewhere during the long Memorial Day weekend. Perhaps, because those events would contradict Mr. Lemons biased narrative.

Anti-Trump written and verbal lies have been totally out of control in the American and foreign media. Actually, no mendacious propaganda is outrageous enough for the media to disseminate it as the unvarnished truth about the President. As The New York Post reported on June 2, 2020, Hillary Clinton published a side-by-side photo of the White House, in which the first was lit up in a rainbow spectrum from 2015, while the second photo appeared almost in pitch black devoid of lighting. Not to be outdone, David Axelrod shared Hillary's photos as "perfect symbolism" of the difference between the former and the present occupant of the White House. Feigning genuine concern for the abysmal state of affairs today, he cried out: "...if ever the country needed the occupant of the White House to shed light, and not heat, now is the time. Sadly, the lights are out."

Upon some investigation by other news outlets, less prejudiced than the inconsolably aggrieved former First Lady, both photos were taken when Barack Obama was the President. Coupled with the narrative of President Trump "hiding in his bunker," this meme attempted to counter Joe Biden's disappearance for 10 long weeks from public view. As the heartrending photos of illegal immigrant children, which were designed to showcase the base cruelty of the Trump Administration, and upon some scrutiny were revealed to have been taken in 2014, when President Obama reigned, the media's depiction of the White House being made a miserable place by the current occupant, is another despicable attempt at ruthless indoctrination.

To demonstrate the hypocrisy and corrupt bent of the Democrat Party and its more extremist followers, it is enough to cite the recent lawsuit brought by The Washington League for Increased Transparency and Ethics, or WASH LITE, against Fox News Channel, its parent Fox Corporation, and two channel distributors, AT&T and Comcast, as well as Rupert Murdoch personally. The plaintiff claimed that Fox News' coverage violated Washington state's consumer protection laws by engaging in a "campaign of deception and omission regarding the danger of the international proliferation of the novel coronavirus." Judge Brian McDonald wrote in his opinion, in which he dismissed the lawsuit, that the public interest group's "professed goal in this lawsuit - to ensure that the public receives accurate information about the coronavirus and COVID-19 - is laudable. However, the means employed here, a (consumer protection) claim against a cable news channel, runs afoul of the protection of the First Amendment." After the judge's dismissal order, Fox News Channel issued the following statement: "Using false portrayal of Fox News Channel's commentary, WASH LITE attempted to silence a national news organization to settle partisan grievances. This was not only wrong, but contemptuous of the foundation of free speech and we are both pleased the court dismissed this frivolous case and grateful to the First Amendment community that rallied to our side."

In brief, the outstanding evil of the so-called liberal media and the various Leftist political organizations, including the current Democrat Party, is that they suffer from absolute and extreme degeneracy, recognize no legal or moral discipline, and practically have emancipated themselves from reality. The journalists and talking heads on the Left of the political spectrum seem to be constitutionally incapable of grasping the organic relationship of words to things. In their imaginary world, the dividing lines between reality and their perceptions are wholly artificial, created maliciously by their enemies. Consequently, they lack respect for facts that lie at the very foundation of communication in a democracy.

Effectively, they think like a Chinese or a Russian. As far as the Chinese are concerned, there is no distinction between reality and the imaginary. Truth is a fantasy. Truth is subjective. The following Chinese proverb will illustrate the Chinese people's relationship to truth: "What is seen is not always the truth." Another Chinese proverb admonishes thus: "One person spreads a lie, ten thousand people spread it as truth." Again another proverb warns: "Do not believe entirely in things and do not completely dismiss them." "There are only two ways to reach the truth - with literature and agriculture." And so on and so forth.

The mirror image of the Chinese attitude toward lie versus truth are the numerous Russian proverbs about the tenuous relationship between these two opposites. The following are some examples. "Lying began with the world and with the world it will die." "Rye beautifies the field and a lie beautifies speech." "A palatable lie is better than a bitter truth." And finally, "Do not mourn for truth - make terms with falsehood."

With the arrival of social media, a ray of hope has appeared on the horizon of institutionalized communication. Suddenly, with the emergence of Facebook, Google, Linkedin, and Twitter, it has seemed to the average person that openness has been clearing up the ideological fog, forced upon the people by the monopolies of mass communicators. The expectation has been that in not so distant future mass communication would be free for good or for evil. Disappointingly, the latter has materialized. What were conceived as "neutral platforms," have been hijacked by the extreme Left whose maxim has been that an ideologically misguided and controlled person is a better subject than an independent thinker and an honest individual. Thus, anyone who has endeavored to argue against or even has criticized the entrenched extremist Marxist ideology of the heads of these platforms, has been stigmatized as a public enemy whom no amount of intelligence and persuasion could save from uncompromising Leftist condemnation.

The latest controversy with Twitter has erupted over President Trump's two tweets about the increase in mail-in voting. He opined thus: "There is NO WAY (ZERO!) that Mail-In Ballots will be anything less than substantially fraudulent. Mail boxes will be robbed, ballots will be forged & and even illegally printed out & fraudulently signed. The Governor of California is sending Ballots to millions of people, anyone...living in the state, no matter who they are or how they got there, will get one. That will be followed up with professionals telling all of these people, many of whom have never even thought of voting before, how, and for whom, to vote. This will be a Rigged Election. No way!" Perfectly valid and fact-based opinion. However, Twitter almost immediately upended both tweets with an exclamation point followed by a link where users of the site could "Get the facts about mail-in ballots."

Clicking on that link, the gullible users of Twitter could read: "Trump makes unsubstantiated claim that mail-in ballots will lead to voter fraud."

Contrary to Twitter's assertion, manipulating mail-in ballots has a very long history. As Real Clear Politics pointed out in a commentary written by Mark Hemingway, President Trump was right and Twitter was wrong. While asserting that "fact checkers say there is no evidence that mail-in ballots are linked to voter fraud, none other than The New York Times cited two studies by CalTech and MIT respectively about the increase in voters' fraud associated with mail-in ballots. An additional problem has been the so-called "ballot harvesting." In 2017, a former Postal Service employee in Texas was convicted of bribery for selling a list of absentee voters to vote harvesters for $1,200. As the commentary further states, Twitter decided to fact-check opinion and not facts. The third offense Twitter committed, according to the commentary, was that it showed clearly its bias vis-a-vis the President. Finally, the author of the commentary accused Twitter that its fact-checking policy lacks clarity and, therefore, it will not be applied in a consistent manner. He concluded that Twitter has employed "political double standards for years."

In the same vein, the New York Post on May 29, 2020, ran an article, authored by David Marcus, under the title "Twitter ignores far worse than Trump - time to stop singling him out." Pointing out first that Twitter flagged a tweet by the President about the riots in Minneapolis, claiming that the tweet "glorifying violence." As the previous commentary, this article states that Twitter "regularly features flat-out propaganda from brutal regimes like China and Iran, and allows the service to be used to crush dissent."

Indeed. As the Jerusalem Post and Haaretz have complained repeatedly, Twitter has allowed the Islamic Republic of Iran, Hezbollah, Hamas, and many other anti-Israel as well as anti-Semitic organizations to call for the destruction of Israel accompanied by calls to the indiscriminate murdering of all Jews across the globe. In addition to these clearly hateful postings, the current avalanche of outrightly false and even libelous tweets about the origin, spread, and nature of COVID-19 have been posted by the Chinese government absolutely unimpeded. The list of these kinds of offensive postings is regrettably endless.

In response, President Trump issued an Executive Order on May 28, 2020. In Section 1 of his order he stated: "Free speech is the bedrock of American democracy. Our Founding Fathers protected this sacred right with the First Amendment to the Constitution. The freedom to express and debate ideas is the foundation for all of our rights as a free people." Then he went on to say: "Online platforms are engaging in selective censorship that is harming our national discourse. Tens of thousands of Americans have reported....online platforms "flagging" content as inappropriate, even though it does not violate any stated terms of service; making unannounced and unexplained changes to company policies that have the effect of disfavoring certain viewpoints; and deleting content and entire accounts with no warning, no rationale, and no recourse."

Section 2 of the Executive Order deals with "protection against online censorship. Invoking Section 230 (c) of the Communications Decency Act, in which it is stated, among other things, that if an online platform restricted access to some content posted by others, it would thereby become a "publisher" of all content posted on its site for purposes of torts such as defamation. Section 3 is designed to "protect federal taxpayer dollars from financing online platforms that restrict free speech. Section 4 empowers the Federal Government to review all unfair or deceptive acts and practices by all online platforms. Finally, in Section 6 the Executive Order directs the Attorney General to "develop a proposal for Federal legislation that would be useful to promote the policy objectives of this order."

There's not a shred of a doubt that President Trump is absolutely right and Twitter is left without a leg to stand on. The only real rationale for democracy is that a tiny non-elected minority cannot pursue policies, which are hostile or even destructive to the opinions, traditions, and morality of the majority. Policies advocated by these mostly single issue groups are foreign and in many instances even repugnant to the majority. Although these groups are free to pursue those ideas and policies as long as they remain within the confines of the laws, they are not entitled to illegally and surreptitiously change the constitution and the laws that they deem being detrimental to their minority ideas and policies. Moreover, respect for the rule of law and the state of the political institutions are indications of how well democracy functions. If these two cornerstones of democracy buckle under the unrelenting assault of those minority groups, they create a feeling of wariness and not confidence. And when uncertainty ensues, chaos is not far away. The experiences of COVID-19 events as well as the most recent Minneapolis riots must serve as unambiguous red flags of the consequences of unprincipled appeasement of those who deliberately undertake to overthrow the constitution, the culture, the traditions, and the moral foundation of the American Republic.

VI. The Multiple Myths of Victimhood in the United States of America and Beyond

Allow me to begin this chapter with a personal note. I was born in Hungary after the end of World War II. My mother's family had to escape Transylvania in 1918, when Romania officially declared its union with the region, which was an integral part of the Hungarian Kingdom for nine centuries. My father was Jewish. His family arrived from Spain via the Holy Roman Empire to Hungary proper at the end of the 16th century. Because of the first explicitly anti-Semitic law called Numerus Clausus passed by the Hungarian Parliament in 1920, two years prior to Mussolini's Marcia su Roma and thirteen years before Hitler became Chancellor on January 30, 1933, he was forced to study medicine in Bologna, Italy. During the war, he was "drafted" to serve in a Hungarian labor battalion, exclusively set up for Jewish men, on the Soviet front. When the Hungarian army retreated, he first was incarcerated in a Ghetto and then sent by the Hungarian authorities to the extermination camp in Mauthausen. He survived and returned to a defeated Hungary. Thus, in the country of my birth, everyone was deemed to be a victim, including the "truncated" state of Hungary.

I was lucky to be able to leave this graveyard of victimhood at a young age. In addition to having been an uncompromising opponent of the Soviet-imposed dictatorship in Hungary, I resented the dishonest mentality that was justified because of the wrongfully inflicted miseries on the nation by all sorts of foreign elements. Because Hungarians felt victimized by the Soviet Union and their minions, they compensated themselves by outwardly demonstrating loyalty toward their masters, while internally they developed an intense loathing vis-a-vis everything Russian. Conversely, they glorified everything "Western." Collectively, Hungarians have led a schizophrenic existence.

However, with every passing year after the pro-Soviet regime collapsed, Hungarians have begun to express ever increasing nostalgia toward the bygone regime and simultaneously badmouth their newly acquired individual freedoms and national independence. Has this condition been a healthy one? Absolutely not. On the one hand, it has deflected responsibilities from the people for their own destinies. On the other hand, it has provided most of the Hungarians with an excuse to dwell on the past and to neglect building a better future for themselves. Therefore, the Hungarian notion of victimhood has always been a sorry collection of vicious circles, without any opportunity for escaping. In brief, Hungarian victimhood has been irredeemably destructive.

Among other national inflictions, the mentality of victimhood has become in the United States of America another political excuse for promoting onslaughts of chaos and anarchy. Fueled by the curse of identity politics, which has facilitated racism that, in turn, has led to the proliferation of violence, the glorification of victimhood has only deepened the already existing divisions within society. Presently, everybody is aggrieved. The individual who feels helpless to influence anything. The group, be it ethnically or racially based, that believes the other ethnic or racial groups are better off, the political organizations that are excluded from the decision making processes by the majorities, the politicians who accuse their counterparts of dishonesty or even illegal manipulations, judges who are powerless against the corrective decisions of superior instances, and bureaucrats who labor under the tyranny of their superiors. They all claim that they were robbed of their free will and that they fell victim to forces that they cannot control.

Yet, most of those grievances are either artificial, self-inflicted, or outrightly criminal. Let's consider the Jussie Smollett story. According to the police report, based on Mr. Smollett's personal account, in the middle of a biting cold winter night in Chicago, when he decided to take a leisurely walk, two white men wearing ski masks and happened to be equipped with a bottle of bleach and a rope that they fashioned into a mock noose, approached him. Supposedly to paint the scene more believable, Mr. Smollett decorated his narrative by claiming that the two white men shouted pro-Trump slogans such as "This is MAGA Country" as well as racist and homophobic slurs.

However, Mr. Smollett's story quickly unravelled. Yet, not quickly enough for the anti-Trump media that cheerfully and uncritically reported the most juiciest details of the alleged assault. Having faced uncomfortable questions as a result of the ongoing investigation, Mr. Smollett decided to play the role of a black and gay victim whose eternal fate is to suffer unjust idignities in the hands of white and straight people. In reality, Mr. Smollett's story unravelled faster than he could continue to spread his lies further. The two white men turned out to be two Nigerian brothers, Ola and Abel Osundairo, who have known Mr. Smollett intimately. Days later, it became crystal clear that Mr. Smollett's story was a total hoax. Having played the race card to its fullest, Mr. Smollett was criminally assisted by the Cook County State's Attorney Kim Foxx who, instead of serving justice, became what Attorney General William Barr rightly termed "dangerous to the public safety." In spite of being a pathological liar like Mr. Smollett, Ms. Foxx was defended by Senators Bernie Sanders and Kamala Harris. For good measure, George Soros showed up in support of Ms. Foxx to the tune of $800,000. By unapologetically promoting a destructive political ideology, Ms. Foxx has achieved only one goal, namely, the total discreditation of Mr. Smollett's bizarre and ultimately fake story. But as in Stalin's show trials in the 1930s, the ideologically loaded narrative was more important than the facts. Apparently, Ms. Foxx and the Senators thought that the show titled "Victimhood" must go on, regardless of the consequences.

Unfortunately, the Smollet story was preceded by many similarly fake accounts of racial violence against black people. Starting with the Tawana Brawley case in 1987, when she claimed that six white men had abducted and subsequently raped her repeatedly, and left her in the woods covered with feces. Again, for good measure, she asserted that the men scrawled racial epithets on her torso. Naturally, Al Sharpton jumped on her story without examining its veracity. Her account unravelled as quickly as Mr. Smollett's. Regardless, even in 1997, Ms. Brawley maintained that "something happened to me."

The strange story of Rachel Dolezal is even more bizarre. "Identifying" as black, while being 100% white, and heading a local NAACP branch, Ms. Dolezal regaled the public with her countless encounters with racist discrimination. In essence, she wanted to be black in order to be a victim. Clearly, she thought her life as a white person was uninteresting compared with the existence of a black individual full of racial tribulations. As her rise to fame advanced uninterruptedly, she must have concluded that being a "persecuted" black person means power and money. Ms. Dolezal's bizarre story played out in the late 1990s when the campaign against "white privilege" had taken off in earnest.

Michael Brown's death at the hands of a white Missouri police officer by the name of Darren Wilson has been a watershed in race tensions for several reasons. The events that led to Michael Brown's death on August 9, 2014, when the police officer noticed that Michael Brown and his friend Dorian Johnson were walking in the middle of Canfield Drive, a busy two-lane street in Ferguson, Missouri, have rapidly become a rallying cry for anti-racism. The story started when officer Wilson asked them to use the sidewalk. Instead of complying with the request, the two young men started to argue with the officer. During the exchange of words the officer noticed a pack of cigarillos in Michael Brown's hand. The officer recalled that a radio dispatcher reported the theft of cigarillos from a market. Then the officer confronted Michael Brown about the cigarillos. As a response, Michael Brown reached into the officer's SUV to seize his gun. A fight ensued. The gun went off. Michael Brown started to run away from the SUV. Then he stopped, turned around, and started to run toward the officer. Michael Brown, a young man with a 6'4" stature and weighing 290 pounds, approached the officer in a threatening manner. Officer Wilson discharged his weapon several times. Regardless, Michael Brown kept rushing toward the officer. Officer Wilson's last shot to the head killed Michael Brown. In Dorian Johnson's version that he shared with a local TV news station, he said the following: "He put his hands in the air. He started to get down, but the officer still approached with his weapon drawn. And he fired several more shots. And my friend died."

Without even superficially checking Dorian Johnson's narrative, the major national television channels, The New York Times, and The Washington Post ran with his story. Ultimately, two separate law enforcement investigations concluded that the two young men robbed the store and that Michael Brown's fingerprints were found on the officer's gun. Moreover, according to both investigations, Michael Brown was not shot in the back but in the front of his torso and head. Finally, the investigation found that Michael Brown did not have his hands in the air when the officer opened fire. Thus, Dorian Johnson's account was totally false. Based on additional information, officer Wilson was not charged with any crime.

Having been incited by Dorian Johnson's false narrative and the equally untrue accounts of the media, an initially peaceful prayer service escalated the following night into a riot. Stores were set on fire. Businesses were looted, damaged, and destroyed. Police officers were pelted with rocks and bottles. The chaos continued unabated for weeks. When St. Louis County Prosecuting Attorney Bob McCulloch announced on November 24, 2014, that officer Wilson would not be indicted, the violent protests started anew. The following spring, President Obama's Justice Department, headed by the then Attorney General "Wingman" Eric Holder, also declined to indict officer Wilson. However, demonstrating the biased mentality of both the President and his Attorney General, the Justice Department issued a report claiming racial bias in Ferguson's policing. Police Chief Tom Jackson and other top officials resigned en mass.

The results of the federal intervention were predictable. Homicides skyrocketed and prospective police recruits were unwilling to enlist with the Ferguson police. Criminals became more arrogant and aggressive. Police officers became more reluctant to enforce the law. Ferguson descended into protracted lawlessness. Mayor James Knowles III of Ferguson put it thus: "There are a lot of people, especially some of the best and brightest, who might have thought they may want a career in policing. They are going to ask themselves the question, 'Do I want to go through this, put my family through this?'" Expanding on the "Ferguson Effect" he added: "When you are not pulling people over, you are not getting these guns off the street, you are not seizing contraband and illegal weapons."

However, Ferguson has become a cause celebre for all sorts of anti-status quo forces. For them mob rule is a welcome instrument in the process of destroying democracy and installing the dictatorship of a small minority. The Freddie Gray case in Baltimore, Maryland, the Eric Garner case in New York City, where he complained that "I cannot breathe," Ahmaud Arbery's cold blooded shooting, and Breonna Taylor's death inside her home by a police officer have radicalized race-based organizations such as Black Lives Matter, the Black Alliance for Just Immigration (BAJI), Antifa, Color of Change, NAACP Legal Defense and Educational Fund, Inc., and UndocuBlack Network. Presently, they all have expanded into a national movement with global ambitions.

The video showing the death of George Floyd in Minneapolis, Minnesota, shocked the conscience of the nation. It also occurred in the middle of the nerve racking CONVID-19 lockdown and the unexpected economic

crisis, resulting in skyrocketing unemployment and extreme financial hardships for around one third of the working population. The sheer intensity,
the rapid escalation, and the aggressive expansion of the violence that has
ensued cannot be explained alone by the undoubtedly senseless death of
a middle-aged black man. Initially chanting the by and large stupid slogan
"No Justice No Peace," the daytime peaceful protests have turned into violent riots at night. Cat Brooks, who co-founded the Anti-Police Terror
Project after Grant was shot dead in Oakland by a BART police officer said:
"It's about Philando Castile, Breonna Taylor and all the other victims, and
about rage by black and brown people that has been going on for many
years. But one thing that's different is that right now, a lot of people doing
these protests are stuck in their houses, lost their jobs, don't know if they
will be able to make a living....This whole thing was powder keg waiting to
explode...Pre-pandemic, it was bad enough. But now that we're in the pandemic, black people are getting messed up even more - getting infected in
bigger numbers than others, having to go to work more than others and get
exposed."

The anti-Trump media have quickly pointed their collective finger at
the President as the ultimate cause of George Floyd's death. As recently as
June 24, 2020, House Speaker Nancy Pelosi asserted that the President and
Senate Republicans are trying "to get away with murder" with their policing reform bill introduced by Senator Tim Scott of Georgia. No wonder
that with every passing day, the late George Floyd has grown in stature as
a martyr of "white racism" and has been depicted almost as a saint. A tall
and heavyset man with a stature of 6"4', weighing over 223 pounds, and
having been a hardened and violent criminal, he has become, after his death,
a pawn in the political power play of the Democrat Party and the Extreme
Left. In reality, he is and will remain a sad example of a broken black culture
that has always prevented the majority of African Americans to emerge
from the dark depths of their victimhood mentality. Correctly, in a letter
to members, Lt. Bob Kroll, the president of the Minneapolis police union,
called George Floyd a "violent criminal." Calling the protesters demonstrating over his death "terrorists," Lt. Kroll condemned the city's politicians for
not allowing use of greater force against them. Complaining that "What is
not being told is the violent criminal history of George Floyd. The media
will not air this." In his remarks, Lt. Kroll alluded to the not so negligible

fact that George Floyd, among other criminal acts, did serve prison time for aggravated robbery with a deadly weapon in the past. Whether Derek Chauvin knew of George Floyd's criminal past is not yet known. However, fact-based news reporting should have made at least a reference to George Floyd's past that included multiple violent felonies and five stints in jail. Moreover, no mention was made of the facts that he tried to pass a counterfeit $20 bill, that his body was loaded with fentanyl, methamphetamine, cannabinoids, and three more drug residues. Finally, nobody pointed out that had he not broken the law and had he not resisted arrest, falsely claiming to be claustrophobic, he might still be alive.

Regardless, as could have been expected, the outrage over Lt. Kroll's letter was instantaneous. From calling him all kinds of names to demanding his prompt resignation, the champions of "truth in reporting" wanted to see blood. Yet, a tweet by Cecilia Regina, a black woman tells the story: "George Floyd was arrested and convicted of robbing and beating a PREGNANT BLACK WOMAN after breaking into her home. He wanted money and drugs and when she didn't have either, he pointed a gun at her stomach." For evidence, she attached photos of the court record of his conviction, as well as his criminal history. In conclusion, she pleaded with the protesters: "STOP MARCHING FOR THIS MAN. Stop posting for him. He was a monster who terrorized BW in life. DO NOT support him with your labor in his death. If you do, you are supporting a man who hated and harmed black women! You cannot have it both ways this time. Either you are for the safety of black women or you are saying that we don't matter compared to black men. Share, share, share."

On June 12, 2020, a 27-year-old Black man named Rayshard Brooks, passed out drunk in the drive-thru lane of a Wendy's in Atlanta, Georgia. His car was blocking traffic, thus restaurant employees called the police. The two policemen woke up Mr. Brooks and asked him whether he had been drinking. When Mr. Brooks answered in the affirmative, the officers proceeded with a normal DUI arrest. Instead of surrendering peacefully, Mr. Brooks started to fight. He wrestled the two officers to the ground and then grabbed a Taser from one of them and tried to use it against Officer Rolfe. When Mr. Brooks raised the Taser to fire, Officer Rolfe shot and killed him.

Again, in spite of these facts, proved by two body cameras, Paul Howard Jr., Fulton County District Attorney, who is an African American, asserted that Mr. Brooks on the night of his arrest was "calm," "cordial," and "really displayed a cooperative nature." Topping his clearly false narrative of Mr. Brooks' behavior, Mr. Howard claimed that Mr. Brooks' demeanor was almost "jovial." A Tweet by Dan Bangino on June 18, 2020, was right on target: Apparently, sleeping in a drive-through on private property, resisting arrest, violently attacking police officers, stealing their taser, & firing that taser at them at close range while fleeing, meets the liberal criteria for 'cooperating' with law enforcement. THIS IS INSANITY." The rest of Mr. Howard's description of the events leading to the tragic death of Mr. Brooks is not worth reciting.

However, it should be sufficient to state that Mr. Howard is a complete disgrace to his elected office. Hastily, he charged Officer Garrett Rolfe with first degree murder and at least ten more criminal offfenses. If convicted, Officer Rolfe could receive the death penalty. Undoubtedly, Mr. Howard has made a purely political decision. Charging Officer Rolfe without being supported by a thorough investigation has nothing to do with due process or the rule of law.

The best illustration against the charges of "institutionalized" and "systematic" racism is the much ado about nothing case of the "noose" found by NASCAR officials in a garage used by half balck half white driver Bubba Wallace. The comic saga of the "noose" that in reality was a small loop tied to the bottom of a rope on a garage door at the Talladega Superspeedway, was designed to make it easier to raise and lower the garage door, and it had been there since at least from October 2019. The whole shamefully and ideologically laden brouhaha about this racist symbol began with a NASCAR announcement that it will prohibit any images or displays of the Confederate flag of future events. Entering the turbulent waters of race politics, NASCAR's leadership self-righteously intoned thus: "The presence of the Confederate flag at NASCAR events runs contrary to our commitment to providing a welcoming and inclusive environment for all fans, our competitors and our industry. Bringing people together around a love for racing and the community that it creates is what makes our fans and sport special. The display of the Confederate flag will be prohibited from all NASCAR events and properties."

After Bubba Wallace's tearful media appearances, multiple shows of solidarity, and NASCAR's leaders righteous indignations, the FBI concluded that the noose was not a racial symbol as hyped by the ideologically biased media. A disbelieving Bubba Wallace initially doubted the FBI's finding that was based on the investigation of no less than 15 agents. Interviewed by none other than the most objective anchor on race relations CNN's Don Lemon, Mr. Wallace expressed his firm belief that the rope was a "straight-up noose." To plead his case further he stated: "I've been racing all my life. We've raced out of hundreds of garages that never had garage pulls like that. So people that want to call it a garage pull and put out all the videos and photos of knots being as their evidence, go ahead, but from the evidence that we have - and I have - it's a straight-up noose." Only after repeated confirmations did he relent and tweeted a statement, in which he said that he is "relieved" to know the "noose" was not meant for him.

Not to be outdone, the relentless champion of anti-racism Al Sharpton confessed that he is still convinced, even against the FBI's finding, that the garage pull is in fact a racist noose. This so-called "Reverend", the tireless apostle of peace and brotherly love, declared on MSNBC: "The FBI identified it as a noose. NASCAR said it was a noose or went along with the FBI's characterization. It was a noose. So, the question is, even if they did not know that Bubba Wallace was going to use that stall, why was a noose in the stall?" Poor Al Sharpton. It appears that the good Lord did not give him sufficient brain mass when he was born. But seriously. As Miranda Devine stated in The New York Post on June 24, 2020, "someone needs to pay the price for NASCAR's noose fiasco." Will NASCAR boss Steve Phelps apologize to all the fans who staged a peaceful protest in their pickup trucks, in the name of his much touted inclusiveness and unity? Will the lying media admit their collective error? Will the Democrat Party disown unbridled hatred masquerading as pure love and selfless patriotism? I do not think that the nation should hold its breath.

The causes and effects of criminality across the globe are vastly different. Specifically, in the United States of America criminality, as every phenomenon in society has been dangerously politicized. Yet, crime data sources tell a more objective story. According to the US Department of Justice, African Americans accounted for 52.5% of all homicide offenders from 1980 to 2008. The rate of Whites was in the same time period 45.3%.

The offending rate of African Americans was almost 8 times higher than Whites, and the victim rate 6 times higher. Most homicides were interracial, with 84% of White victims killed by Whites, and 93% of African American victims were killed by African Americans. Blacks have accounted for almost 70% of homicides committed with guns. In their vast majority, Whites homicides were non-gun offenses. Interracial violent victimizations (excluding homicide) cases between Blacks and Whites, as of 2018, totaled 593,598. Out of these cases Blacks against Whites amounted to 537,204, 90% of all the known crimes. On the other hand, Whites committed 56,394 crimes against Blacks, less than 10% of all cases.

In the wake of the COVID-19 pandemic, the recent riots intimate the desire of extremist and radical minorities to force a great new orientation locally as well as globally. These as of yet loosely organized and in their ideological orientations diverse groups' ultimate objective is to facilitate a violent "revolution" that would overthrow the existing system and replace it with the dictatorship of a small minority. Slogans like "No Justice No Peace," "Black Lives Matter," "#Defund The Police," "Breathing While Black," "Down With White Power," "Stop White Supremacy," and a cornucopia of violent invectives against the police indicate that their imagined road to this "revolution" leads through the destruction of the rule of law. Calls to defund and even abolish the police departments entirely have been gaining support in the media too. An organization by the name "Working Families Party" that claims to be a part of the Democrat Party, calls for "significant, permanent reductions to existing policing and carceral infrastructures." Another representative of this organization pontificates about "the punitive impulse (the police) embody saturates nearly every facet of American life," where officers "take the place of social workers and emergency medical personnel and welfare case workers, and when they kill, we let them replace judges and juries, too." To up the ante, a Brooklyn College sociologist Alex Vitale demands the total abolition of all police forces. This anti-police propaganda and incitement generalize an unattractive view of all police departments across the nation and depict police officers as savages, who are always ready to shed black people's blood joyfully. Attacking or even killing policemen has become an honorable act of protest against representatives of the "racially oppressive criminal justice system." Ironically, these champions of racial equality, racial tolerance, and respect for the rule of law, are determined to deny the same rights to anyone whose skin color does not correspond to theirs.

Apparently, when it does not fit the Black Lives matter agenda, blacks killed by blacks do not really matter. At the early stages of the riots, on May 30,2020, a Federal Protective Service Officer was fatally shot and another officer was critically injured outside a U.S. courthouse in Oakland. The murdered officer was the 53 year old David Patrick Underwood, an African American. On June 2, 2020, David Dorn, a 77 year old retired St. Louis police captain, also an African American, was shot dead "protecting his friend's pawn shop from looters during the protests." Stephan Cannon, a 24 year old black person was charged with first degree murder in this case. Moreover, he was charged with burglary, robbery, armed criminal action, and being a felon in possession of a firearm. Another black man, the 27 year old Jimmie Robinson was charged with armed criminal action, stealing and unlawful possession of a firearm, and burglary.

To add an additional dose to the burgeoning idiocy of these organizations, Black Lives Matter wants to establish an armed branch of "peace officers" to allegedly combat police brutality in black communities during the so-called "war on police" campaign, according Peter Aitken of Fox News. Aitken's report quotes the New York chapter chairman of Black Lives Matter Hawk Newsome thus: "We're talking about self-defense. We're talking about defending our communities." Moreover, he said: "You know what it's like to see a taser pointed at a 7-year-old, you know what it's like to see a 67-year-old black woman...pepper sprayed and pushed to the ground?" And then this sentence: "We are preparing and training our people to defend our communities." He finished his description of the "peace officers" corp thus: "We pattern ourselves after the Black Panthers, after the Nation of Islam, we believe that we need an arm to defend ourselves...We will build and train peace officers to keep the peace in our communities, to defend our communities, to keeo our communities safe." His words are nothing but a call for arms. Asked by Martha MacCallum of Fox News Channel on June 24, 2020, what he hopes to achieve through violence, this righteous night of social justice responded first with a diatribe against America's alleged violent history, and then stated: "If this country does not give us what we want then we will burn down the system and replace it."

Kneeling down by police, marching in riots with extremist elements, and declaring solidarity with people determined to destroy everything is definitely not the solution. Symbolized appeasement gestures have never worked against extremism. It might deescalate tense situations momentarily but are absolutely inadequate to solve the genuine problem of black criminality in society.

Politically, by creating lawlessness, they aim at weakening and eradicating the achievements of over 240 years of American history. Yet, one of the cornerstones of individual freedom based democracy is a legal system that is founded on the independence of the judiciary. Once prosecutors change individuals and judges issue verdicts under mob pressure, democracy is destroyed too. The destruction of the legal system is always followed by fear, panic, chaos, and anarchy. Also ironically, the first to be gripped by those sentiments are the destroyers. The chaos and anarchy they themselves created overwhelm them first. The result is always ruthless terror and ubiquitous genocide.

There is nothing in common, therefore, between reform and destructive revolution. Reformers do not want to destroy everything from top to bottom. They do not want to overthrow the Republic but to improve it. In total opposition, today's American revolutionaries and their foreign comrades want to establish through violence a revolutionary state, in which lawless terror shall eliminate every notion of humanity.

The United States of America and the overwhelming majority of its people have become the unwitting victims of a tiny minority's victimhood revenge. If this majority will succumb to the violence of this minority, the country will first endure countless calamities, including political, economic and financial collapse, and then the wholesale annihilation of American civilization. The poisonous myths of minority victimhood, so dear to the destructive elements of society and so enticing for their guilt-ridden fellow travellers, must be decisively countered. These two intermingled trends completely distort the meaning of freedom and the fundamental principles of democracy. By confounding rightful grievances and violent anarchy, instead of distinguishing between them, as should have been done long ago to keep the reasonable minds balanced and clear sighted, office holders of both parties have done a terrible disservice to this great country.

From generation to generation an ever increasing number of politicians and intellectuals have been working assiduously in spreading the confusion to every corner of the United States of America and to every layer of society. What is this confusion all about? It consists of the erroneous belief that it is sufficient to pay lip service to the founding principles of the country, while suffocating justified grievances in the bottomless depths of indifferent equanimity. By refusing to give an exact definition of the problem, by constantly equivocating about its ambiguities, the American people have ended up attributing to the periodical eruption of spontaneous anger political and intellectual legitimacy.

It is not very difficult to ascertain why this omission gained momentum. The eruptions of anger are swift. Few weeks, occasionally a few days are needed, provided that circumstances are favorable. Reforms, on the other hand, require time and joint efforts that are slow and in many times cumbersome, and even painful. Thus, oversimplification is by far less complicated than hard mental and practical work. Destruction is far less laborious than construction. Inventing a strategy for the long term requires assiduous work. Acting out one's emotions without control is more self-satisfying. This latter destructive thaumaturgy now in fashion has popularized the notion that it is easy to change existing political principles and even economic laws, or to invent new legal ideas. These appear to be far more important than the consequences that they will create, namely, chaos, anarchy, and inevitable despotism.

An even more destructive idea is reparations for past slavery. Voices in the African-American communities advocating slavery reparations in the trillions of dollars have multiplied since George Floyd's death in Minneapolis. As recently as June 3, 2020, Black Entertainment Television (BET) co-founder Rober Johnson called for "wealth distribution" to "create growth" and as an "atonement" for slavery to the tune of $14 trillion. In this context, he opined "Now is the time to go big. We need to focus on wealth creation...and to do that we must bring the descendants of slaves into equality with this nation."

Speaking of "bringing the descendants of slaves into equality with this nation," one should not ignore the developments that led up to the Civil Rights Act of 1964, as well as the history of the last 50 years. After the Civil

War, three amendments were added to the constitution. The 13 Amendment abolished slavery. The 14 Amendment made the former slaves citizens. The 15 Amendment gave all men the right to vote regardless of race. In practice, however, many states - particularly in the South - used poll taxes, literacy tests and similar measures to circumvent the constitution and keep African American citizens basically disenfranchised. Strict segregation was enforced through "Jim Crow" laws. In 1957, Congress established a Civil Rights Section within the Justice Department, coupled with a Commission on Civil Rights to investigate discriminatory practices. In 1960, Congress moved to authorize court-appointed referees to assist blacks register to vote.

The Civil Rights Act of 1964 entered into force on July 2, 1964. Generally speaking, the Act banned segregation based on race, religion or national origin from all places of public accommodation, including courthouses, parks, restaurants, theaters, sport arenas, and hotels. Title VII of the Act forbad discrimination on the grounds of race, religion, national origin, and gender by employers and labor unions, and created an Equal Employment Opportunity Commission with the power to file lawsuits on behalf of aggrieved workers. Moreover, the act disallowed the use of federal funds for any discriminatory program, authorized the Office of Education (later the Department of Education) to assist with school desegregation, provide additional authority to the Commission on Civil Rights, and prohibited the unequal application of voting requirements. Subsequently, the Act was extended to include disabled Americans, the elderly and women in collegiate athletics under its legal protection.

This Civil Rights Act was followed in quick succession by the Voting Rights Act of 1965, and the Fair Housing Act of 1968. The first prohibited literacy test and similar discriminatory practices, while the latter banned discrimination in the sale, rental, and financing of property. The Equal Credit Opportunity Act of 1974, outlawed

discrimination by creditors against applicants on the ground of race with respect to any aspect of a credit transaction. The Community Reinvestment Act of 1977, limited redlining, namely, the systematic denial of various services by federal government agencies, local governments, as well as the private sector, to residents of specific neighborhoods or communities, either directly or through the selective raising of prices.

In 1987, the Civil Rights Restoration Act mandated that all recipients of federal funds must comply with civil rights. The Civil Rights Act of 1991 extended the court system to trial by jury in employment discrimination lawsuits. The Violent Crime Control and Law Enforcement Act of 1995, instructed the U.S. Sentencing Commission to increase penalties for hate crimes. The Emmett Till Unsolved Civil Rights Crime Act of 2007, opened the door to African Americans to initiate the reopening of criminal cases of violent nature committed before 1970, to be reopened. Finally, Matthew Shepard and James Byrd Jr. Hate Crimes Prevention Act of 2009, allows federal authorities, including the Federal Bureau of Investigation, to investigate and prosecute hate crimes.

Federal court decisions in the second half of the 19th century manifested varied interpretations of both the relevant amendments and congressional legislation. The Slaughterhouse cases in 1873, limited the enforcement of the Privileges and Immunities Clause. The 1876 decision in the United States v. The Cruikshank case ruled that the Bill of Rights did not apply to state governments. The United States v. Reece in the same year narrowed the interpretation of the Fifteenth Amendment. Plessy v. Ferguson in 1896, ruled that racial segregation and Jim Crow laws in the South to be constitutional under the "separate but equal" doctrine. Williams v. Mississippi in 1898, upheld voting restrictions in the 1890 Mississippi State Constitution. Cummings v. Richmond County Board of Education in 1899, upheld de jure segregation in schools. Yet, several court decisions ruled that grandfather clauses and all white primary elections in the South are unconstitutional.

The celebrated Brown v. The Board of Education case, actually composed of four cases, overturned segregation in schools and the separate-but-equal doctrine. Lucy v. Adams desegregated the University of Alabama. Boynton v. Virginia in 1960, decreed that segregation in public transportation was illegal under the Interstate Commerce Act of 1887. McLaughlin v. Florida overturned Florida's ban on interracial cohabitation. Harper v. Virginia State Board of Elections in 1966, abolished the poll tax in state elections.

Executive orders and proclamations, beginning with President Abraham Lincoln's Emancipation Proclamation in 1862, through President Harry S. Truman's 1948 Executive Order No. 9981, that desegregated the U.S.

Armed Forces, and President Richard M. Nixon's 1969 Executive Order No. 11478, that prohibited discrimination on certain grounds in the competitive service of the federal civilian workforce, were the most important milestones on the way of enforcing the constitution and the laws of the country.

The legacy of gradual progress in eliminating discrimination against blacks is undeniable. Those who had fought for full equality did it by invoking the Judeo-Christian notion of egalitarianism. They did all point out that both Judaism as well as Christianity celebrate every human creation to be equally the sons and daughters of God. Moreover, for them the existing inequalities inherent in the societies were creations of imperfect individuals, subordinated to the welfare of the human soul. In this context, they were more concerned about the fundamental question of how to bring about changes in laws and institutions for good? They knew that changes only work in conjunction with the culture, the customs, the religion, the morality, the traditions, and the political as well as economic interests of the times they lived in.

Martin Luther King realized these truths. He acknowledged that lawfully organized social movements have the constitutional right to present their grievances, to promulgate their desires, to fight for new laws, or to argue against retrograde legislation. He also recognized that the minority could be wrong. Its views could only be legitimized when those views express the will of the majority. In this spirit he declared in 1966: "We are going to have this kind of vigorous protest. My hope is that it would be non-violent. I would hope that we can avoid riots because riots are self-defeating and socially destructive."

Martin Luther King had been right! Riots are self-defeating and socially destructive! Because he believed in the United States of America, he wanted to keep the country united. Because he wanted to keep the country united, he advocated the unity in equality of all its members. But where does this national unity originate from? Again, Martin Luther King had the vision of the unity of rights and obligations. In this context, he asked himself: Upon what are these rights and obligations founded? Upon violent force? His answer was an unambiguous No. No, because he firmly believed that violent force cannot establish enduring rights or responsibilities. Violent force is always short-lived. Clearly, Martin Luther King strived to create permanency in the nation as well as in human relations. For this reason, he understood that violence cannot create enduring rights when it is imposed on the majority by force through a minority. Therefore, he argued vehemently against the use of violence. He comprehended that violence cannot be permanent, and when it seizes, the rights thus acquired will also disappear. Consequently, he concluded that only by consensus within society could permanent changes be affected.

Another maxim stipulates that every human problem has at least two sides. It means that even if the majority desire peaceful changes but the minority disagree and are determined to achieve radical transformation by violent means, the former will surely defend against the display of extreme brutality. Since no person or group of people are perfect, one has to ask the question that is hardly ever raised: What is wrong with the African American community? At the root of the malady of the African American community and its members is the condition of the black families. The family composition of African Americans has been a nagging national problem for at least a century. However, the first comprehensive study was only published in 1965, by Daniel Patrick Moynihan. Named after his author this study, called a Report, examined the correlation between black poverty and family structure. Its main thesis was that the ongoing destruction of the Black nuclear family structure will be a major impediment toward political and economic equality. When Moynihan's report came out, the out-of-wedlock birth rate was 25% among Blacks. In 1991, this number jumped to 68%. In 2011, 72% of Black children were born to unmarried mothers.

In 1968, the Research on the African American Family book, written by Robert B. Hill, concluded that the single-parent homes would be the undoing of the African American people. In addition to listing the strengths of the black family structure, he also dwells at length on the weaknesses inherent in this truncated family structure.

The alarming breakdown of the Black family structure was also depicted by Bill Cosby. In his book, co-authored with psychiatrist Alvin Poussaint, Come On People: On the Path From Victims to Victors, they write: "A house without a father is a challenge. A neighborhood without fathers is a catastrophe." The authors point out that mothers "have difficulty showing a son how to be a man" and that this difficulty presents a problem when there are no father figures around to show boys how to channel their natural aggressiveness in constructive ways. They also hypothesize by asking the question: "We wonder if much of these kids' rage was born when their fathers abandoned them." Moreover, they assert that single mothers, angry for having abandoned themselves, habitually transfer their rage and hatred to their sons. They cite curses like "You're stupid," "You're an idiot," "I am sorry you were born," or "You'll never amount to anything."

Cosby's book was followed by the movie The Blind Side in 2009. Based on the 2006 book with the same title, the storyline features Michael Oher, an offensive lineman who was drafted by the Baltimore Ravens of the National Football League. The movie presents the life story of Michael Oher from homelessness to his adoption by a white family. As his story unfolds, the viewers learn about the heartlessness and utter irresponsibility of the mother and the fact that he never really learned who his father was.

Woefully, Moynihan's Report, Cosby's book, and Michael Oher's biography are no exceptions. What was depicted even in the 1960s as the "traditional" American family, does not exist any more. A recent study by Professor Zhencho Qian of Ohio State University bemoans the fact that the family unit is not central to Americans in the "marriage-go-round" culture. His conclusion is that "there is no longer any such thing as a typical American family." Yet, existential stability starts at the family home. Without it, instability, uncertainty, and even wariness could engulf the individual and all those who are related to him or to her. When such a condition becomes universal, society will suffer. Indeed, there is a direct correlation between the health of democracy and the health of the micro-family unit. Existential uncertainty in a family means lack of trust in the fabric of society. Under such conditions, any crisis, as for example the COVID-19 pandemic with its associated calamities, can easily spill into a general demonstration of discontent with the status quo.

Clearly, the solution is to strengthen the fabric of micro-families. In this quest, the failed experiences of the past should be taken into account. Primarily, money is not everything. Albeit, it is very easy to shower money on a problem, but without a sound strategy, the money so generously spent on a problem will evaporate while the problem itself will continue to grow exponentially. After having spent north of $22 trillion on helping African Americans, the results are unsatisfactory. Mainly, because of lack of leadership by the cities and communities that have been charged with managing the money. The list of failed mayors and city councils is as long as the length of the United States of America. Coupled with the abysmal state of public education where teachers' unions are concerned more about job and financial security for their members rather than educating children, these local potentates clearly have failed the people who elected them. The more effective approach would be to restore, preserve and strengthen the Judeo-Christian culture of America. The Judeo-Christian religion has always been key to the spiritual well-being of the American nation in general and the African American community in particular. To combat the moral decline of the black youth, it is imperative to fight the lies of the most radical elements within the black community, specifically the absolutely deranged narratives of the bogus social justice/white supremacy cannons. Such a strategy would definitely benefit black communities and nourish democracy in the United States of America and across the globe too.

In crass opposition, Black Lives Matter published a Manifesto under the title "WHAT WE BELIEVE." In its entirety it is an incoherent, illogical, and basically stupid piece that does not amount to a viable strategy. After reassuring the reader of the Manifesto that "We make our spaces family-friendly and enable parents to fully participate with their children," the next paragraph adds to the fake intellectual confusion: "We disrupt the Western-prescribed nuclear family structure requirement by supporting each other as extended families and "villages" that collectively care for one another, especially our children, to the degree that mothers, parents, and children are comfortable." Complete idiocy. Did anyone inform the authors that "collective care for one another" was tried in the Soviet Union and throughout its empire in Eastern and Central Europe with devastating consequences? Did anyone call the authors' attention to the fact that the number of abandoned children caused the largest youth criminality in the Soviet Union in human history? Did the authors really contemplate their proposal in light of the actual misery of the black families? The answers are unequivocally no. For this reason, this Manifesto cannot be taken seriously. It is nothing but pseudo intellectual garbage.

VII. The Collective American Insanity

The twin crises that have befallen the United States of America in January and in early June of this year respectively have been characterized by their comprehensive devastations. Although the causes of both crises appear to be extremely complex, their common roots are very simple. These common roots can be summed up as follows: The cause of the chaotic disorder, which has wreaked havoc on the United States of America and throughout the world, is not so much the international instability among the various nations and organizations, but is the result of something more profound. It is the internal vulnerability of countless governments in general, and the crisis of democracy in the United States of America in particular. The COVID-19 pandemic now devastating the world is itself the result of the internal instability of the People's Republic of China, its ruling Communist Party, and the destructive incompetence of Xi Jinping's failed leadership. His and his colleagues' deliberate and essentially evil decision to unleash the novel coronavirus on the rest of the world has convulsed practically not just Asia but all the other continents too. Hence, the significance of the questions that must be answered: What do all these internal convulsions mean? Where are they heading to?

As far as the United States of America is concerned, the answers to these questions are political. Since their independence, the American people had been aware of their unique position. Hence, the notion of American exceptionalism had been born. Beyond the two Oceans, with the gradual end of the era of colonialism in the rest of the world, the newly liberated nations have been forced to learn how to govern themselves. Then, all over these states the same tragedy has happened. Colonialism collapsed but most of these states could not find a republic. In almost all of these states, weighed down by colonial traditions, chaos and anarchy have prevailed leading to the establishment of overwhelmingly despotic regimes.

In Central and Eastern Europe, the post-Soviet decades have shown similar political and economic equivocations. From the quasi-legitimate dictatorship in Hungary, sanctimoniously labeled by its Prime Minister Viktor Orban as illiberal democracy, to the fledgling republics in the rest of the formerly Soviet occupied states, the prestige of democratic governance has been rapidly declining. With this phenomenon, the opposition in every state has been weakened systematically, and sooner rather than later is bound to disappear. Everywhere the people have less and less respect for their governments, for the simple reason that the latter are only interested in power and money for themselves.

Presently, the world consists of live volcanoes that are ready to erupt at any moment. The customary lethargy and indifference of the people are dissipating and entire continents are becoming ripe for revolts. Encouraged by weak leaders and fragile governments, the spirit of revolt is gaining strength globally. The most significant manifestations of this spirit of revolt are the worldwide protests against the alleged institutionalized and systematic racism in the United States of America and on behalf of Black Lives Matter. Across the globe, these revolts cause mayhem and violent destruction, while their participants with scant education claim, rather disingenuously, that they possess the best ideas to solve all the ills of the world. This ubiquitous insanity has propagandized its value by attacking everything that for centuries had undergirded human civilization, including the glorious past as well as the political systems of the present and the future, beginning with individual freedoms and popular democracy.

Among the political groups and movements, the most violently revolutionary are those that congregate around ethnic, nationalistic, and religious ideologies. The common premise is their attacks on the alleged nefarious conspiracies by all governments to stifle their rights, freedoms, and equality, and more generally, to enslave, despoil, and impoverish the masses. This abusive and violent opposition to the status quo in the United States of America, armed with failed and destructive Leftist ideologies, appears to drive the narrative globally.

Undoubtedly, these political, anarchistic, and even militaristic groups and movements are not intelligent or earnest. The glue that holds them together is unbridled hatred against the status quo, unrestrained hunger for absolute power, and uninhibited craving for money. Among these attributes, wealth is their great passion that, paired with ruthless cruelty, has recently set the United States of America and the rest of the world on fire. More globally, the people who comprise these groups and movements are only pawns by the Chinese Communist Party, the Kremlin, and other unsavory despotisms, which want to preserve their rotten regimes by bringing down democracy in the United States of America.

The contradictions and untruths that have been inherent in these radically violent groups and movements in the United States of America, as they have enjoyed relative impunity, have given rise to widespread social confusion, because they have been based on nothing but momentous lies. To prevent the exposure of these groups' and movements' intellectual poverty, politicians of all colors and the overwhelming majority of the media have created a virtual Tower of Babel, in which everyone has spoken only his or her garbled language, without listening to or trying to understand anybody else. In this cacophony of incoherent voices, assorted minorities within the nation hope to engineer fundamental political and social revolutions.

Revolution! Revolution! Revolution! From times immemorial, revolutions been staged by the governed against their governments. Revolution also meant reorientations of civilizations, sciences, and human thoughts, that had fundamentally altered history. However, what is propagated by Black Lives Matter and other like minded groups and organizations, including the Democrat Party, is designed to completely overthrow the constitution and the entire legal system of the United States of America by ruthless violence, and replace them with chaos, anarchy, and mob terrorism.

The American Constitutional Republic is in danger. The real victim is the country and at least 80% of its inhabitants. The main and common responsibility of all office holders in the Union should be to "support and defend the Constitution of the United States against all enemies, foreign and domestic; that I will bear true faith and allegiance to the same." For more than two weeks now, the United States of America has been the victim of violent and senseless criminal acts by the enemies of the Republic and for everything it stands. Officeholders who have caved to violent intimidation through conviction, opportunism or fear, and have decided to shirk their oaths and responsibilities, do not deserve their offices. For them, the honorable gesture would be to resign en masse. In the alternative, they all should be voted out, because they betrayed the trust of their electorate.

The world had always been imperfect. Accordingly, no person or government is perfect. The fatal tragedy of George Floyd's untimely passing is that those who now exploit his death have acted under two fundamentally flawed myths: the myth of institutionalized and systematic racism, and the myth of being on "the right side of history." As perhaps the worst president in American history has repeatedly stated: "My fellow Americans, I am confident we will succeed in this mission (one can insert any subject here), because we are on the right side of history." Unfortunately, Barack Obama never stopped there by always adding the following alternative about being on "the wrong side of history." Again, never illuminating the essence of these two alternatives, he has contributed to the fallacy of both myths, so dear to all those radical and extremist groups and organizations.

The common intellectual idiocy of Obama's and his fellow travellers' thinking is that like Karl Marx and his followers they perceive history as a linear development toward an ever more perfect universe. Yet, progress has never been easy to create and then to preserve. Moreover, progress has not always been a positive force in history. History has always been very complex and, therefore, highly contradictory. Viewing history, including the present, as former President Obama and his adherents have been doing with their amateurish benefit of 20/20 hindsight, as an unavoidable progression toward universal happiness and aplenty, is to deny the role of humans in shaping the past, the present, and the future of mankind. Beside, those who think of government as inherently bad, must recognize that it is not omnipotent. Existing governments, be they democracies or dictatorships, can only set minimum conditions for social peace and stability. This, however, is exactly where the complications begin, because minimum conditions will not always suffice. Politics is not just an idealized system of actions and reactions. On the contrary. Mostly it is a complex system of administration of laws and rules by elected and appointed individuals. Harmonizing sometimes contradictory actions and reactions in order to strike a proper balance is very difficult. Whether we in the United States of America have done a poor or relatively good job of preserving and improving this balance is open to question.

Yet, the present chaos and anarchy surely will not solve anything. Destroying the political foundation of the Union and its legal system for a utopian and, therefore, clearly unworkable orientation of government and society is irresponsible, and outright idiotic. Yet, the Democrat Party has put its future in the hands of a deceptively good-natured, but visibly demented career politician, who has allowed himself to be captured by the most radical and extreme groups and movements. Joe Biden and his Party are trying to appease everybody, in particular the lower and middle classes. These tactics do not amount to a set of coherent political strategies. Momentarily, some previously credentialed Republicans are also rallying to his side.

Yet, Biden defeating the incumbent President is highly unlikely. Come November, the majority of the voters will realize that what Joe Biden and the Democrat Party are trafficking in are a bunch of fables and lies. For it has been the senseless violence of their core supporters and not the President or the Republican Party who have caused the riots, in order to fabricate for Joe Biden a feckless majority. The latter, however, is not the mandatory of the national will but the faithful tool of the Democrat Party. Solid political power is not rooted in violent intimidation. Joe Biden's present support is conditional on his moving his campaign further toward reckless extremism. By doing so, he will lose the votes of the vast majority of Americans who expect their President to spare the nation from sliding into immediate onslaught and anarchy. Politics that is based on these occurrences is negative and fueled by nothing but brazen hatred. Moreover, as soon as order is reestablished, hateful rhetoric loses its deceptive value and its relevance is wiped out entirely. Surrounded by strong constitutional institutions, Joe Biden and the Democrat Party will not achieve their objectives.

The United States of America and the rest of the world are at an inflection point. The vast majority of the world population are not philosophers. Neither are they blessed with intelligent intuition that might guide them toward good decisions. Appallingly, politicians on the federal as well as the state and local levels are frequently misguided in their evaluation and reactions to important events. Their intellects are routinely blinded by opportunistic considerations or oblique ideologies and, for these reasons, they fail to understand the interconnectedness of social phenomena.

The massive political storm engulfing the United States of America and the rest of the world is frightening, because it is loaded with vicious lies and alluring illusions. In these confusing times, in the United States of America, politicians of diverse persuasions at all levels have attempted to justify their political existence by two contradictory principles. On the one hand, they have professed legitimacy based on their electoral victories. On the other hand, they have claimed to be entitled to follow their own selfish interests in direct contravention of their electoral mandate.

The consequences of such an equivocal posture are predictable. These politicians are condemned to hover between two unrealities, corrupt governing and spineless survival. No democracy can endure long under these negative circumstances. When political power pretends to be active when it is paralyzed by its own faults, it becomes a mere fact without the political support that is essential for its effectiveness. Thus, because these politicians attempt to maintain power by propagating two prohibitively detrimental contradictions, essentially absolute lies, they permanently violate common sense and the moral sensitivity of their voters. Ergo, they compound their devious duplicity by hiding their true intentions.

For illustration, let's take the case of the liberal news site Slate claiming that "violence" is an "important tool of protest." For good measure, Slate included a 24-minute audio analysis about "the history of violent protest." Stating that "Big structural change in America doesn't happen without violence," the audio glorifies violence, to use Twitter's favorite slogan to censor the President of the United States of America.

In the same spirit, Nicole Hanna-Jones asserted in New York Times Magazine that the destruction of property "is not violence." Doubling down on her idiotic comment, she avered in an interview with CBSN that the George Floyd protest should be interpreted differently: "I think we need to be very careful with our language...Yes, it is disturbing to see property being destroyed, it's disturbing to see people taking property from stores, but these are things." Warming up to her topic, she continued thus: "And violence is when an agent of the state kneels on a man's neck until all of the life is leached out of his body. Destroying property, which can be replaced, is not violence. And to put those things - to use the same language to describe those two things I think really - it's not moral to that." Hanna-Jones, who recently won the Pulitzer Prize for her extremely biased and mostly inaccurate portrayal of slavery that started, according to her in 1619, did not stop there: "...any reasonable person" would discourage the destruction of other people's property but not in "these unreasonable times." Proving that her idiocy knows no limits, she continued: "So when we have people who say that people should respect the law, they're not respecting the law because the law is not respecting them. You can't say that - that regular citizens should play by all of the rules when agents of the state clearly are not." Thus, according to this radical genius, throwing out the baby with the bathwater is good, because the demise of George Floyd justifies the elimination of everything good in an orderly society.

The list of Democrats and non-affiliated extremists glorifying senseless rioting, looting, and even killing of those who try to protect their livelihood is long. Amid the two major crises, Nancy Pelosi's biggest problem is the removal of 11 Confederate statues on display throughout the Capitol complex. Thus, she sent out a letter saying that the statues in question "pay homage to hate, not heritage," and demanded that they be removed. The 11 statues consist of Jefferson Davis of Mississippi, Wade Hampton of South Carolina, John E. Kenna of West Virginia, General Robert E. Lee of Virginia, Uriah Milton Rose of Arkansas, Edmund Kirby Smith of Florida, Alexander Stephens of Georgia, Zebulon Vance of North Carolina, Joseph Wheeler of Alabama, and Edward Douglass White of Louisiana. Contrary to the Speaker's claim, these individuals are part of the heritage of the United States of America. Those who demand the prompt and uncritical removal of their statues are driven by revenge and hate. Moreover, such an act of retribution will not further reconciliation and unity - topics that allegedly are so dear to tender-hearted Democrats and their coterie of faithful voters. Finally, a nation that arbitrarily erases a part of its history, because a minority demands it, will end up without history, culture, traditions, and a worthy political and legal system.

Massachusetts Attorney General Maura Healey came up with this gem of idiocy: "Yes America is burning, but that's how forests grow." These are the words of a high elected official who campaigned on a law and order platform. Another genius de jour of the Democrat Party Representative Maxine Waters, Democrat from California, proved the umpteenth time that her place is not in the House of Representatives but in a mental institutions: "Young people, they have a whole new definition for "looting." "They say "looting" is predatory lending in, you know, minority neighborhoods, where they're paying 300 and 400 percent more on loans by these payday lenders."

Her soulmate in Seattle Teresa Mosqueda, justified the wholesale destruction of property in her town thus: "Colleagues, I hope we're all saying we understand why that destruction happened and we understand why people are upset." Taking to heart her call to arms, her colleague Tammy Morales opined: "But what I don't want to hear is for our constituents to be told to be civil, not to be reactionary, to be told looting doesn't solve anything." "It does make me wonder why looting bothers people so much more than knowing that across the country black people are being killed."

Another depository of excessive brain-power CNN's Chris Cuomo demanded to know: "Please, show me where it says that protests are supposed to be polite and peaceful." Clearly, he never heard of the First Amendment.

Amanda Mull of the Atlantic ranted on Twitter that "If you build a society that exhausts and abuses people and privilege capital over human life, I'm not sure which other imaginary 'civil' options you expect people to exercise."

Encouraged by the irresponsible statements of their elected representatives, a group of protesters in Seattle declared the establishment of the "Capitol Hill Autonomous Zone." Comprising six blocks around the abandoned Precinct building of the police, the group posted a sign saying that "You are now leaving the USA." To calm the nerves of those who disagree with them, Code Pink wrote on Twitter: "Without the police, the zone has turned into a peaceful George Floyd memorial filled with art, positivity & love." The question is only for how long? The answer came within hours after the declaration of the Autonomous Zone in the form of a list of demands. In a blog post on Medium published recently, the protesters outlined the necessary "policy changes for the cultural and historic advancement of the city of Seattle." Claiming to be the voice of the "Collective Black Voices," the protesters demand the outright abolition of both the Seattle Police Department as well as the court system.

Not being satisfied with the destruction of the police and the judiciary, the protesters added: "This means 100% of funding, including existing pensions for Seattle Police." "At an equal level of priority we also demand that the city disallow the operations of ICE in the city of Seattle." While demanding impunity for themselves, the protesters also demand that the federal government prosecute past police brutality to the full extent of the laws.

Moreover, they demand the immediate release of everybody arrested for marijuana and resisting arrest offenses. In addition, the protesters demand the "degentrification of Seattle" and a "decentralized election process," whatever these two foggy demands may mean. Finally, in the fields of health and human services they call for hiring more black doctors and nurses who would specifically take care of black patients. In education, the protesters demand anti-bias training for all educators, a greater focus on Black and Native American history, and the removal of any Confederate statues throughout the state.

Instead of mitigating the conflict, the occupiers of the so-called Autonomous Zone aggravate it. Reports about them starting to extort money from local businesses for "protection" have reached the police and city politicians by the thousands. The lame reaction of the Seattle police is advising those who complain to call 911 for help. Good luck. The same police that had to vacate the area, because politicians did not want to excite more the extremist thugs. The lesson is unambiguous: A conflict between two irreconcilable forces can only be resolved by a unitarian solution. The return to the status you ante by the amalgamation or the extermination of the lawlessness. In this case, there is no third way.

Demonstrating the misleading power of a lie, Seattle Mayor Jenny Durkan ventured to say on CNN's Chris Cuomo, that the occupiers are a "block party," rather than thugs who committed "an armed takeover." "We've got four blocks in Seattle that you just saw pictures of that are (sic) more like a block party atmosphere. It's not an armed takeover, it's not a military junta. We will make sure that we can restore this, but we have block parties and the like in this part of Seattle all the time, it's known for that." Adding another lying insult to inhuman injury, Durkan added: "There is no threat right now to the public. And we're taking that very seriously. We're meeting with businesses and residents. But what the President threatened is illegal and unconstitutional. And the fact that he can just tweet that and not have ramifications is just wrong."

Unfortunately, reality again caught up with the idyllic narrative of the elected American idiots of the West Coast. On June 19, 2020, a shooting erupted that left at least one person dead and another critically injured. The police and the ambulance service van were not allowed to enter, lest they would witness for themselves the paradise that was established in the center of the city.

Moreover, Mayor Durkin is wrong on both accounts. The Constitution as well as federal laws provide the President with the legal authority to call up National Guard units or even the Military to stop illegal acts that prevent the enforcement of federal laws. When violence exceeds the resources of state and local authorities, the federal government is obligated to protect the states "against domestic Violence," at the request of the legislature or the governor. Article I, Section 8 authorizes Congress to "provide for calling forth the Militia to execute the Laws of the Union, suppress Insurrections and repel Invasions." In the Insurrection Act of 1807, Congress authorized the President to use troops in response to rioting that rises to the level of insurrection that "opposes or obstructs the execution of the laws of the United States or impedes the course of justice under those laws." The crushing of the Whiskey Rebellion in 1794, the deployment of federal forces against the Confederacy between 1861-1864, the positioning of the 101st Airborne in Little Rock, Arkansas in 1957, and the use of the military in Los Angeles in 1992, are sufficient examples of the President's and the federal government's constitutional powers.

To up the ante, Webster, Massachusetts Police Chief Machael Shaw prostrated himself by laying face-down on the pavement in front of the Black Lives Matter protesters. He stayed in this position for exactly 8 minutes and 46 seconds, the same amount of time Minneapolis police officer Derek Chauvin held his knee on George Floyd's neck.

Not to be outdone, Kentucky Governor Andy Beshear wants to provide 100% health coverage to every single black resident of his state, allegedly "to end health care inequalities." Usurping the authority of the Supreme Court, Beshear declared that "health care is a basic human right."

On June 6, 2020, a photo was posted. In the photo, two happily smiling young women hold up a sign that reads: "This is for Donald you big Fat Orange nasty smelling, fat Bitch! Why you took away our Mother Fuckin' rights with your triflin dirty Orange racist ass big Fat bitch! Oompa loompa body ass bitch!" No comment is needed.

Deeply repentant Virginia Governor "Blackface" Ralph Northam is busy trying to remove Confederate monuments. However, his intent to get rid of Confederate General Robert E. Lee has been temporarily stopped by the courts. Richmond mayor Levar Stoney rushed to join the party. He announced that he will seek the removal of the other Confederate monuments along Monument Avenue, which include statues of Confederate President Jefferson Davies and Confederate Generals Stonewall Jackson and J.E.B. Stuart among others. Not waiting for Mayor Stoney's ordinance, a group of protesters toppled the statue of Confederate General Williams Carter Wickham in Monroe Park. Photos and video from The Richmond Times showed that red paint was splashed or sprayed on the statue.

In the nation's capital, Mayor Muriel Bowser has repeatedly clashed with the President over the stationing of the National Guard in the city and re-naming streets around the White House. Senator Mike Lee of Utah issued a statement on June 5, 2020, that read: "Evicting Utah National Guard personnel from their hotels after a late-night shift risking their lives to protect Washington is a shameful, petty, discrediting decision by Mayor Bowser." President Trump also criticized the Mayor: "The incompetent Mayor of Washington, D.C., @MayorBowser, who's budget is totally out of control and is constantly coming back to us for "handouts", is now fighting with the National Guard, who saved her from great embarrassment over the last number of nights. If she doesn't treat these men and women well, then we'll bring in a different group of men and women."

Michigan Governor Gretchen Whitmer, who has gone beyond her legal authority to impose the harshest lockdown measures and to prevent people from assembling, was pictured shoulder-to-shoulder protesting with a large crowd. While claiming that she did not violate against her own order, the text of her order attests to a different interpretation: "Persons may engage in expressive activities protected by the First Amendment within the State of Michigan but must adhere to social distancing measures recommended by the Centers of Disease Control and Prevention, including remaining at least six feet from people from outside the person's household."

New Jersey Governor Phil Murphy suggested that protesting against police brutality were more important than destroying the livelihoods of business owners.

Al Sharpton intoned in the presence of George Floyd's family members: "George Floyd's story has been the story of Black folks. Ever since 401 years ago, the reason we could never be who we wanted is you kept your knee on our neck. We were smarter than the underfunded schools you had us in but you had your knee on our neck. We could run corporations and not hustle in the street but you had your knee on our neck." Falsification of history, disgusting distortions and bald-faced lies that Al Sharpton has regularly trafficked in since the Tawana Brawley rape fiasco.

But more significantly, the myth of victimhood. Black people are not responsible for anything. Everything is the fault of the devilish white race. For their sins, whites must pay eternally through their noses, in order to keep black people content and happy. Otherwise, black people are entitled to murder, loot, destroy, and not to be good citizens.

Examples of such irrational and even outrageous ideas abound. As a consequence, young blacks have not been taught a system of inviolable and imperative rules, establishing rights and wrongs. They have not been explained by their fathers and their mothers the rights and responsibilities of good citizens, law abiding Americans, rights and duties of federal, state, and local governments, as well as rights and duties of parties, voluntary organization, and haphazardly assembled groups. To their juvenile way of thinking and beliefs, they have been absolved of being good citizens, be-cause they have been victimized by the bad white majority. Have not elected and self-appointed demagogues, such as African American office holders as well as Al Sharpton and company, have told them every hour of the day that the United States of America is the most racist nation on earth for not letting them as a minority run the Republic? Such a false "transformism," also advocated by former President Barack Obama and his wife, has been nothing but a pretext to shirk assuming responsibility for the enduring mis-ery of a segment of the black people. These so-called elected and self-an-nointed representatives of the African American minority have been trying to fool everybody, including themselves. For these reasons, their passionate hatred befogs their intellect. As a result, the thus misled people are blinded to the realities of their actual situation and their place within their families, communities, as well as the nation. A tragedy and even a catastrophe that have prevented this great nation to be united by the common principles of the constitution.

Even more sadly, the Nelson Mandela Foundation has come out endorsing the use of violence by Black Lives Matter to achieve political goals. In a statement released in early June 2020, it is claimed that a "growing rage" against white supremacy justifies the violent destruction of lives and property across the globe. Arguing against "to readily dismissing" violence by criminals and extremists, the statement reasons that violence can be the result of deliberate calculation by communities who "see that only such action elicits the desired response from the state." Moreover, "When communities are confronted by both resilient structural violence and attacks on their bodies, violent responses will occur...The use of violence can be rational and carefully targeted." So much for the legacy of Nelson Mandela, the first democratically elected President of South Africa.

What all these persons and organizations do not comprehend is the gradual rise of resentment to their arrogant and highly aggressive rhetoric and actions. Yet, it could be predicted with almost absolute certainty that a backlash is building by the majorities to counter the violent and unreasonable bullying of the single agenda minorities within society. Clearly, chaos and anarchy cannot be tolerated for long. An eye for an eye and a tooth for a tooth mentality had always led to mutual hatred and protracted violence. Politicians and public figures who justify or even glorify violence should think about the immorality of hatred, limitless retribution, and senseless violence, before they open their mouths. The same should apply to the overwhelming majority of the official and social media.

Yet, the grievance industry is a global phenomenon. However, no state and no government confronted with lawlessness shall tolerate its destruction. Criminal laws had always served a deterrent function in every society. Since the turn of the 20th century, the notion of rehabilitation, as the Gladstone Report of 1895 stated "rehabilitative ideal," has also gained ground. However, this idea has always had its limitations. Experiment and practice have forced both theoreticians and practitioners of criminal laws to rethink how far rehabilitation can go. Against hardened criminals and violent thugs rehabilitation rarely works. Therefore, those who murder in cold blood and destroy property the full severity of the penal codes shall be applied. Only this way can peace and stability in every society be protected and maintained.

VIII. The United States of America: The Dream of the Past, Present, and Future

In Book 6 of Plato's Republic he relates a conversation between Socrates and an Athenian citizen Adeimantus, in which the former points out the imperfection of democracy by comparing the Athenian state to a ship. To illustrate his point, Socrates asks Adeimantus a question: If you are heading on a journey by sea, who would you ideally want deciding who will be in charge of the vessel, just anyone or people educated in the rules and demands of seafaring? The latter, of course, answers Adeimantus. Socrates agrees and continues questioning his compatriot. So why then do we keep thinking that any person should be fit to judge who should be the ruler of a country? Socrates' argument is twofold. On the one hand, running a country requires more than the mere fact of citizenship. It calls for statesmanship, a unique quality that can only be acquired by education and life experiences. On the other hand, voters also must be taught how to be thoughtful citizens, who are capable of electing the right people to the various public offices.

The state delegates to the Constitutional Convention 1787, in Philadelphia Pennsylvania, were appointed by the original states. Overwhelming number of the Signers were educated men. William S. Johnson of Connecticut was the president of Columbia College, formerly known as King's College. Richard Bassett of Delaware was instrumental in the organization of the Judiciary of the United States. William Few of Georgia was the director of the Manhattan Bank and the president of City Bank. Daniel Caroll of Maryland oversaw the construction of the federal capital. Rufus King of Massachusetts was a Senator and Minister to England. John Langdon of New Hampshire was a Senator and a governor. Jonathan Dayton of New Jersey became the Speaker of the House. Alexander Hamilton of New York was the principal author of the "Federalist Papers" and the first Secretary of Treasury. Richard D. Spaight of North Carolina was a three-term governor of his state. Benjamin Franklin of Pennsylvania needs no introduction. Charles Pinckney of South Carolina served both as a governor as well as a Senator. George Washington and James Madison of Virginia became

Presidents of the United States of America respectively. A number of outstanding individuals, such as Richard Henry Lee, Partick Henry, Thomas Jefferson, John Adams, Samuel Adams, and John Hancock did not accept delegation or could not attend the Convention. These Founding Fathers, who were visionaries, truly laid the foundations for the remarkable progress of the United States of America. Without their and their successors' enormous contributions, America could not have become the current sole superpower of the world.

Education in general and self-improvement in particular were the most prominent ambitions of the new Republic. In spite of their political differences, the Founding Fathers were in agreement that only an educated person could really be free. Individual freedom as a prerequisite to build a democratic society were writ large in the Declaration of Independence as well as across the seven original Articles of the Constitution and its first ten Amendments of 1789.

Yet, the Constitution came into being as a document conceived by imperfect humans. It was exceptional in its vision of a stable and peaceful society but not a perfect legal construct. The first ten and then the following seventeen Amendments have been proof that circumstances change as societies progress. In order to adjust the system of government and the rights and responsibilities of the citizenry to these changing circumstances, new thinking and corresponding solutions were needed. Human history, and American history is no exception, has been replete with the never ending quest for perfection, because this struggle is endless.

Slavery was the single most important issue that fundamentally ran counter to the general premise of ubiquitous human freedoms and equality. It was implicitly permitted in the original Constitution through Article I, Section 2, Clause 3, known also as the Three-Fifths Compromise, which regulated how each slave-holding state within the Union can count its slave population into its total population for the purposes of appropriating seats in the United States House of Representatives and direct taxes among the states. It took a protracted Civil War and then one hundred more years to begin rectifying an obvious injustice in the fabric of American constitutional order. Yet, final victory might be outside the realm of human ability. However, to give up on righting a fundamental injustice would be wrong, because it will mean the long term ruin of the American dream for everybody inside and outside the United States of America. Democracy without universal human rights lacks credibility. Individual freedoms without educated citizenry are imperfect. Political legitimacy tainted with contradictions is tenuous.

Conversely, when opposition to imperfections is blinded by infinite hatred, it becomes destructive and, therefore, extremely dangerous to the stability of a democracy. When such infinite hatred is abused or even cynically exploited for nefarious political purposes, everybody affected by the disastrous opposition will suffer. Ruthless violence, irresponsible calls for the overthrow of the elected governments follow. The culmination of all these catastrophic actions is character assassination, politicization of the judiciary for pseudo-legal manipulations, and outright terror.

Amid the formidable challenges of the COVID-19 pandemic and the resulting worldwide economic crisis, the United States of America is facing the challenge of destructive political extremism, disguised as protests against so-called "institutional and systemic racism." In spite of the fact that their idol Martin Luther King warned against destructive violence as "...a way of achieving racial justice is both impractical and immoral. It is impractical because it is a descending spiral ending in destruction for all. It is immoral because it seeks to humiliate the opponent rather than win his understanding; it seeks to annihilate rather than to convert. Violence is immoral because it thrives on hatred rather than love," barely educated and mostly young people believe that the only way to achieve social justice/human rights is through the senseless terrorization of the entire nation.

Racially justified violence is also self-defeating because it is based on self-hatred. It teaches blacks to hate themselves and also all the other races. It declares everything, including gender, parents, family, religion, country, and history contemptible and ultimately toxic. Indeed, what is happening in the United States of America and also across the globe has nothing to do with constructive opposition but everything to do with despotism. Employing extreme violence rarely seen before, is unacceptable and must be rooted out relentlessly. For protesters and rioters to burn schools, to set fire indiscriminately to police buildings and non-public buildings, to tear down statues and to demolish historic memorials, and taking private property by force, is terrible and totally unacceptable.

Fundamentally, the peaceful or the violent disturbances of the present have very little to do with the death of George Floyd or the economic hardships caused by the COVID-19 pandemic. More significantly, they are the results of the long simmering identity crisis within the African American communities. This identity crisis, in turn, is the direct consequence of identity politics gone awry. Coined by the Combahee River Collective in 1977, the term identity politics referred to a political perspective for racism, sexism, heterosexism, and classism. The movement's aim was to focus on the plight of marginalized and oppressed groups for social justice and political liberation.

The historian Arthur Schlesinger Jr. opined in his 1991 book The Disuniting of America that identity politics is necessarily divisive and detrimental to the unity of liberal democracy. He argued that "...movements for civil rights should aim toward full acceptance and integration of marginalized groups into the mainstream culture, rather than...perpetuating that marginalization through affirmation of difference."

In the same vein, Brendan O'Neill stated that identity politics only creates schisms along lines of a particular identity. "[Peter] Tatchell also had, in the day,... a commitment to the politics of liberation, which encouraged gays to come out and live and engage. Now, we have the politics of identity, which invites people to stay in, to look inward, to obsess over the body and self, to surround themselves with a moral forefield to protect their worldview - which has nothing to do with the world - from any questioning."

With that O'Neill touched upon the crux of the problem. Identity politics forbids for minorities assimilation and revels in their uniqueness, through which they absolutely reject any compromise with society's laws, morality, culture, and traditions. Their justification of moral superiority is as self-defeating as false. Self-defeating, because it freezes their identity in the present and the past, thus preventing any progression in the future. False, because the objective of every society is to preserve and strengthen the spiritual unity of the nation and not to recklessly experiment with, modify, or even destroy it.

Moreover, those who adhere to the concept of identity politics believe that human relations in a democracy are one-way-streets. And because they are misunderstood and oppressed, the majority has a moral obligation to always yield to their demands, however defective they might be. Such mentality not just excludes but expressly forbids any assimilation of minorities within any given society. Nations, in particular democracies, are in tumult when governments, which are legitimized by majorities, start yielding through never ending appeasements to exaggerated and often misleading social justice/human rights rhetoric.

In this manner, these minorities turn themselves into destructive political forces. Deep down in their hearts and minds they know that their ideas are not winnable, because the majority of society cannot identify with their narrow minded agenda. The only way for them to maintain political relevance is to constantly threaten the majority through violence.

For all these reasons, the present policies of the federal as well as the majority of state governments, and most of the local municipalities are wrong. By kicking the proverbial can down the road, they have been creating victims on both sides of the political spectrum. In this way, every member of the American society feels entitled to become an executioner of everyone who opposes his or her beliefs.

At the end, the opposing forces will create a catastrophe. Such a tragic outcome can be avoided by electing politicians who understand how to make productive use of their legal powers. For that to happen, the people must obtain objective and not biased information from the electronic as well as the written media. Indoctrination must also be fought in the schools and institutions of higher education. The barrage of disseminating lies as truths by so-called journalists and teachers must be countered decisively. Only a well-educated citizenry could make correct decisions. Otherwise, the same citizenry will remain shut within a multitude of vicious circles, which first will weaken and then ultimately destroy the United States of America.

The present disturbances and riots are only the beginning of the impending catastrophe. A catastrophe, which if not countered decisively, will stretch out over one or more centuries. Presently, elected governments on the federal as well as the local levels are attempting to do everything possible to satisfy the marauding minorities. For many elected officials, Black Lives Matter, Antifa, and like-minded groups have become the political fashion. Everyone desires to understand their grievances, regardless how idiotic they might be. Everyone pleads for patience and calls for flattering them. Everyone believes, against all odds, that only this way could the peaceful future of the nation be secured.

Of course, most of such arguments are nonsense or outrightly idiotic. The right of opposition in a democracy does not include the use of violence in the service of attempting indiscriminately to achieve political objectives. Lamentably, in the United States of America, the destructive opposition appears to be much stronger than the constructive one. This destructive opposition has worked hard since 2016, to destroy the prestige of the presidency, of the federal government, its secretaries, the Congress, the judiciary, the electoral majority, the religious organizations, the economy, and the constitutional pillars of democracy. As a result, respect for the past, the present, and the future of the country has declined discernibly.

The death of George Floyd has triggered the spirit of revolt, which has engulfed almost the entire country. Today, the feeling of impunity encourages especially the ultra revolutionary elements to attack everyone and everything - the President, his administration, Congress, the military, the police, the banks, the industry, and the majority, accusing them all to be a part of a secretive conspiracy to deny them their freedom and equality. They are particularly violent in assaulting Whites, Republicans, and Jews. This destructive opposition, stuffed with pseudo-Socialist and even little understood Marxist-Leninist-Maoist gibberish, advocates policies that are clearly hostile to the United States of America, its democracy, its past and present, its culture, and its traditions.

The lies and contradictions that have been inherent within these destructive opposition forces have given rise to elected officials who have demonstrated on a daily basis their own identity crises. The most egregious case remains the disgusting hypocrisy of Virginia Governor Ralph Northam. This despicable human being was caught after his election to have allowed his photograph, in which he poses with a black face in the company of a fellow student wearing a KKK outfit in his medical school yearbook page to be published. Following long days of deafening silence, he finally resurfaced and promised to do "the hard work" of atonement and apology to restore his moral and political standing with the people of his state.

To add insult to injury, Governor Northam experienced an epiphany and claimed brazenly that the individual in the photograph with the black face was not him. This blatant lie was refuted by another simultaneous revelation and acknowledgement that on a different occasion he wore shoe polish on his face for a dance contest in 1984, in San Antonio, after graduating from medical school. To make things even worse for the Governor, it was also revealed that one of his nicknames in college was "Coonman."

Amidst the ubiquitous uproar over these racist manifestations, the Governor stated that he is determined to stay in office and to cling to his desk, in order to redeem himself. To demonstrate his newly found humility, Governor Northam promised to hire a private investigator to find the truth about the yearbook photo, which he identified as "not me." Needless to say that he never hired such a person. In this manner, the Governor's embarrassing fiasco was never cleared up.

Yet, the Northam story has not ended there. Virginia's Democrat Lieutenant Governor Justin Fairfax, an African American, who would have succeeded the Governor, had his own problems. This seemingly fine example of an upcoming African American Democrat was also accused of sexual assault by an African American college professor. Finally, Virginia's Attorney General Mark R. Herring, also a Democrat, who would have been in line to replace the Lieutenant Governor, wore blackface to a party as a college student in 1980 too, according to his own admission.

But let's go back to the Governor. In the wake of his duplicitous behavior, a tsunami of demands for his resignation ensued. Even The Washington Post, which has been in the tank for Democrats forever, published several pieces calling for his immediate and unconditional resignation. Yet, the Governor was serious about personal redemption. Having captured both Houses of the Legislature in 2018, the Democrat Party of Virginia has embarked on the road for black forgiveness. Led by the immutable Governor himself, who miraculously transformed himself into a repentant white Santa Claus for the African American minority in his state, the Democrats in both Houses have fast tracked legislation to appease their Black constituency. From tax relief to African American families to prioritizing laws that echo the political demands of Black Virginians, the Governor's forgiveness campaign has been in the highest gear. Whether such a campaign of self-redemption on the backs of Virginia taxpayers is the right way to govern a state remains open to interpretation.

Yet, before the curtain has been drawn on this sorry melodrama, the Governor performed a last prostration act at the Virginia Union University, a historically Black college. In exchange for promising to continue "the conversation regarding a path to move forward" and "to begin to develop a plan to reach healing and reconciliation," the Governor got the blessings of Professor Cornel West of Harvard, former Richmond Mayor the Reverend Dwight C. Jones, and the University President Hakim J. Lucas. This story would have been worth being depicted by the Italian poet Durante di Alighieri degli Alighieri (referred to as Dante) in his Divina Commedia (in English the Divine Comedy).

Another fine example of hypocritical deportment is the aforementioned Professor Cornel West. According to his Wikipedia page, "he is an American philosopher, political activist, social critic, author, and public intellectual. The son of a Baptist minister, West focuses on the role of race, gender, and class in American society and the means by which people act and react to their 'racial conditionedness'." To enhance further the confusion of this manifestly contradictory description, the Wikipedia page added the following sentence: "A radical democrat and democratic socialist, West draws intellectual contributions from multiple traditions, including Christianity, the black church, Marxism, neopragmatism, and transcendentalism." A renaissance man for all seasons or a charlatan? The question is up for individual interpretations.

Yet, examining Professor West's views more critically one cannot escape the impression that his rhetoric is unabashedly a toxic mixture of dogmatic, rigid, and uncompromising Marxism-Leninism-Stalinism-Maoism. His doctrinaire "philosophy" is coated in the artificial mannerism of religious humility, which makes him more palatable to some conservatives too. Weighing in on the ongoing protests and riots in reaction to George Floyd's death in police custody, he opined that "black faces in high places" were unable to facilitate needed changes, because they all succumbed to the "capitalist economy" and the "militarized nation state." Thus, a purely doctrinaire Marxist interpretation.

Then comes the carrot to the gullible conservatives: "The Black Lives Matter movement emerged under a Black President, a Black Attorney General, and a Black Homeland Security (Secretary) and they couldn't deliver."

Then, again the doctrinaire Marxist: "It is a lynching at the highest level. No one can deny that," referring again to the death of George Floyd.

To fully unload on the United States of America, he continued thus on CNN: "I think we are witnessing America as a failed social experiment. And what I mean by that is that the history of black people for over 200-something years in America has been looking at America's failure."

No Professor West! Not exactly! It is not solely America's failure that the black communities deliberately and consciously have refused to be assimilated. Waves of refugees for innumerable countries and with fundamentally different cultures have successfully integrated into the American "melting pot." After almost $23 trillion investment, affirmative action, wholesale appeasement, the misery of the black communities is clearly disheartening. However, blaming America for the African Americans' obstinacy to assimilate is an assertion beyond the pale. Such a rhetoric only cements the decision to stay outside the mainstream of American society and cry wolf whenever black nonconformism clashes with the rule of law, morals, and traditions of the majority. America is not "a failed social experiment." The failure of the black communities to assimilate cannot serve to denigrate the over 240- years accomplishments of the greatest country on earth.

In the same CNN interview on May 30, 2020, Professor West went on ranting: "Its capitalist economy (meaning America) could not generate and deliver, in such a way that people could live lives of decency. The nation state, its criminal justice system, its legal system could not generate protection of rights and liberties." Again, his assertions are outrightly untrue. No country's economy is more open, more successful, no state's criminal justice system provides more protection to lawbreakers, and no society offers more rights and liberties than the political, legal, and social institutions of the United States of America.

Professor West must be forgiven for not having experienced the "blessings" of dictatorships, authoritarian regimes, and naked despotism. Regardless, he closed his macabre interview with a sanctimonious statement: "And I thank God that we have people in the streets. Could you imagine this kind of lynching taking place and people are indifferent, people don't care, people are callous?" Finally, he delivered his coup de grace: "The system cannot reform itself." Again, his opinion is untrue. Experiment proves that the history of the United States of America is a continual progress toward the dream of an ever better society. Moreover, does this damning sentence mean that only the violent overthrow of the Republic is the solution? Does his parting sentence suggest that he is for a Leninist-Stalinist-Maoist Revolution in the United States of America? Are his sanctimonious views the solution for the misery of the majority of black people? Certainly not. The solution should be assimilation into the welcoming American "melting pot."

In another interview with Chris Wallace on May 31, 2020, in the name of unbiased reporting, Professor West was questioned about his views at Fox News broadcast. Again, he said: "What we're seeing here is the ways in which the vicious legacy of white supremacy manifests in organized hatred, greed and corruption." When Chris Wallace, as usual, did not challenge him, Professor West went on to say: "We're witnessing the collapse of the legitimacy of leadership, the political class, the economic class, the professional class, that's the deeper crisis." Again, not an objective and unbiased analysis but idiotic rubish. And such an unserious scholar teaches at Harvard!

Another moron in the guise of pious religious devotion is Alfred (Al) Charles Sharpton Jr. As founder of the National Action Network, the self-described civil rights activist, Baptist minister, talk show host and politician, has spewed hatred against all non-black people since his national appearance on behalf of Tawana Brawley. Not the one to miss any chance to loudly disseminate his false doctrines, Mr. Sharpton was the main speaker at George Floyd's memorial service on June 3, 2020. As reported by all the networks, he went after "White America" with a vengeance. For starters he intoned that "George Floyd's story has been the story of Black folks." Warming up to his subject he continued: "Ever since 401 years ago, the reason we could never be who we wanted is you kept your knee on our neck. We were smarter than the underfunded schools you had us in but you had your knee on our neck. We could run corporations and not hustle in the street but you had your knee on our neck." He is a fraud who has become rich by playing the gullible politicians and rich people like a fiddle for money, in order for them to remain in his good graces. In reality, he is nothing but a con man.

The essence of the narrative of the Obama presidency is tragic. Having won the 2008 elections against an extremely weak and emotionally unstable Republican Senator John McCain, Barack Obama exhausted himself by fighting two demons simultaneously. On the one hand, he rose to the presidency by promising to change the way politics worked in Washington, D.C. and beyond. On the other hand, he failed decisively in his efforts, because he lacked both the intellect and the experience to fundamentally transform American society. The result was equivocation, stagnation, and meaningless speeches that were designed to substitute for actions. Desirous to " bend the arc of history," he ended up accomplishing nothing. Except for the symbolic value of having been the first Black President, Barack Obama merely bided his time and completely withdrew from both domestic and foreign policy issues, including dealing in a meaningful way with the relative backwardness of the black communities. Declaring often that he is on "the right side of history," he literally abandoned his presidency to the fortuitous vagaries of an anomalous history.

Since his presidency depended on bold solutions that he repeatedly promised, Barack Obama was a failure for Whites and Blacks alike. Instead of the titanic efforts that he pledged, he delivered empty platitudes. Tragically, Barack Obama's tenure was also characterized by attempting to justify his administration's existence through the uniqueness of his persona, toward which the majority of the American people, rightly or wrongly, remained by and large lethargic. This hedonistic approach to governing upset the fundamental principle of democracy, according to which legitimacy should ascend from below and authority should descend from above. Barack Obama accomplished one thing - the almost total paralysis of the federal government.

Nothing positive came out of his presidency. Oscillating between his Marxist interpretation of history, which always has been fallacious, and his ingrained narcissistic hedonism, Barack Obama as the 44th President was an unmitigated disaster. The expected reconciliation between the races was all for naught. Instead, his failure has given rise to a new monster, the leaderless and desperately hateful mob. Like Barack Obama, members of this mob do not know what they are protesting or rioting for. Yet, today, this mob terrifies the entire world, because it mainly terrorizes itself.

Barack Obama's legacy, both domestically and internationally, is nothing but an appalling jungle of paradoxes and intellectual incompetence. Instead of having harmonized the old and the new, he bungled the mediatory and conciliatory forces of American government, thus unleashing the contradictory and even violent elements of society. At the end of his presidency, Barack Obama was neither identified with his Democrat Party nor with the minorities to whom he largely owed his elections.

The misfortune on the current domestic and international atmosphere is that, instead of mitigating the tensions, it aggravates them. By their very nature, these tensions are immune to half-hearted measures. Only decisive unitarian decisions will enable societies to return to unity of purpose. Hence, a government that does not lead only contributes to the general confusion. A government that pretends to be effective when it is not, becomes discredited. The inexorable ending of such corrupt governance is that the system becomes not credible. More importantly, nothing is gained by unprincipled compromises, because they are, with rare exceptions, incomplete, unsatisfactory to all sides, and ambiguous. Basically, the Democrat Party's solutions are false. Alternatively, President Trump should apply, without hesitation, the rule of law that the overwhelming majority of the American people support.

From a political perspective, a qualified majority is a clear strength of the Union. This signifies that the President must be the champion of the constructive majority and not the destructive minority. The reason for that is the absurdity of a situation, in which the minority supports the sovereign desires of the people as long as the latter submissively forfeits its political free agency. In this case, democracy dies and the Union perishes. What Joe Biden and the Democrat Party advocate is an illusion of democracy that would result in a national catastrophe.

IX. A Global Perspective

The history of the United States of America could be summarized in two phrases: buoyant self-confidence, coupled with utopian-like optimism. This positive and boundless optimism enabled the country to turn most of its dreams into realities and to create the greatest nation on earth. Domestically, this successful outcome was accomplished through many hardships and even more contradictions. Internationally, the United States of America emerged as the sole superpower in a constantly restless and occasionally deeply troubled world.

Throughout the last two and a half centuries it also attempted, in good faith, to give the rest of the world the instruments of sovereignty and democracy. More often than not, the rewards were bitter disappointments and cynical scorn. As soon as the American government handed over to the new foreign governments the instruments of their new sovereignty, most of them used it to thwart the institutions of democracy, and force their people into the bondage of dictatorship, authoritarianism, and despotism. It was this Sisyphean quest for ubiquitous freedom and democracy that became the enduring fate of the United States of America across the globe.

To be politically the strongest and militarily the most powerful nation came laden with onerous responsibilities. Among those, the main responsibility was to maintain the image of a domestically progressive, yet stable country. In order to achieve these often contradictory conditions, every government since the presidency of George Washington relied on the democratic principle of majority legitimization. The repeated wish of these dynamic majorities was that their governments should govern within the constitutional limitations of the Republic and its morality and traditions. However, since the Great Depression and the subsequent unusually long presidency of Franklin Delano Roosevelt, it has become increasingly difficult to apply the principles of the constitution within all three branches of the federal and local governments.

After the collapse of the Soviet Union, the United States of America, its allies, and its friends have remained without a major foe. Following a short hiatus of international stagnation, September 11, 2001, occurred. As a consequence, NATO has embarked on the treacherous campaign of uprooting Islamic terrorism. The unity of political resolve was again interrupted by the subprime mortgage crisis of 2007-2008, also known as the global credit markets contraction and insolvency crisis of investment banks and other financial institutions. The incoming Obama Administration lacked even a semblance of a coherent domestic or foreign policy. Internationally, President Obama's two terms in the White House must be characterized by unnecessary and humiliating appeasements as well as by never ending injurious misjudgements of the global reality. For these reasons, Obama's presidency, both internally and externally, was permanently convulsed in the paroxysms of incompetence-driven fear and unexpected spasms of pseudo-creativity. The final result of his shamefaced reign was the rapidly deteriorating quality of the American political culture.

The so-called "Russia Collusion " and the multiple investigarions that followed, culminating in the impeachment of President Trump should never have happened. Former President Obama's crusade first against General Michael Flynn and later against his successor in the White House started in April 2014, when Flynn was forced out as the head of DIA following his disagreement with the administration's policies over the war in Syria, the rise of ISIS, and generally over Obama's incoherent tactics in the greater Middle East.

On July 31, 2016, the FBI opened the Crossfire Hurricane probe into possible ties between then candidate Trump's campaign and Russia. The probe initially focused on George Papadopoulos, a low level participant in the campaign. On August 15, 2016, two FBI employees Peter Strzok and Lisa Page had their now infamous text exchange about having an insurance policy just in case Trump should be elected. "I want to believe the path you threw out for consideration in Andy's office - that there's no way he gets elected - but I'm afraid we can't take that risk. It's like an insurance policy in the unlikely event you die before you're 40," wrote Strzok to his secret lover.

The next day, the FBI opened a sub-case under the Crossfire Hurricane umbrella codenamed Crossfire Razor targeting Flynn and his "inappropriate" Russian contacts. Again, on the next day, August 17, 2016, FBI and DNI provided Trump and his presumptive National Security Adviser Michael Flynn with the first briefing, including on Russia. At the same meeting James Comey the then Director of the FBI surreptitiously slipped in an agent posing as an assistant to secretly observe Flynn for a new investigation. According to the Justice Department's Inspector General Michael Horowitz, "SSA 1 told us that the briefing provided him 'the opportunity to gain assessment and possibly some level of familiarity with Flynn.'"

Crucially, on September 2, 2016, Page texted Strzok about Obama's expressed desire to be closely informed on everything the FBI is doing on the Russia "collusion" case: "POTUS wants to know everything we're doing." On November 10, 2016, just two days after Trump won the election, Obama told his successor that under no circumstances should he hire Flynn as National Security Adviser.

On January 3, 2017, the two lovers discussed in several text messages the possibility that, because of Flynn, the incoming President should not get unrestricted briefings. However, the next day, the lead agent in Flynn's Crossfire Razor probe recommended the case to be shut down for lack of derogatory evidence. What followed could have been a textbook process in a banana republic. From Strzok's repeated unlawful interventions to keep the probe against Flynn alive, through Obama's and his loyal political hacks' illegal actions, and to the politically nefarious conspiracy of the unholy alliance of the Clapper-Comey-Brennan triumvirate to carry out a coup d'etat against the duly elected President of the United States of America, they did their utmost best to destroy the Trump presidency from its start. The fake "Russia Dossier" authored by former MI6 agent Christopher Steele, financed by the Clinton campaign, and used extensively by the FBI to obtain at least four FISA warrants to keep the investigation rolling, were all mired in lies, deceptions, outrageous hoaxes, and revolting illegalities.

The enormity of former President Obama's and his political appointees' brazen attempt to overthrow the results of the 2016 presidential election cannot be overestimated. In the first time in American history, an outgoing President undertook to undermine, obstruct, and fatally paralyze his successor's presidency.

To fully understand Obama's and his comrades' crimes, one has to comprehend the true meaning of democracy in a constitutional republic. In this context, the government owes its legitimacy and thus its existence to free elections by the majority of the voting citizenry - in the case of the United States of America to the majority of the electors. The goal of such elections is to ensure a peaceful transition of power and to protect the constitutional order of the nation. Therefore, the ultimate objective of every election, especially the presidential one, is to strengthen the unity of the nation through continuity and not to destroy the legal process by overthrowing illegally the results of the constitutionally mandated elections.

History teaches us that when either elected or appointed officials abuse the constitution and the entire legal system of a nation, that nation and, in the case of the most powerful one, the whole world would face grave dangers of succumbing to chaos and anarchy. The previous 20th century was marred by the reigns of two destructive ideologies, which emerged from the ruins of failed attempts at democratization. From the devastations caused by the 1917 Bolshevik Revolution and the Nazi takeover of Germany in 1933, the European continent still has not fully recovered. Sadly, it may not recover at all.

Throughout the ordeals of the last century, the United States of America remained true to its founding constitutional principles, namely, that the people should decide which vision they would embrace and which ideas they would reject as against their beliefs, morality, and traditions. The losing party became the constructive opposition. Hence, the nation has grown stronger by every presidential election. Former President Obama's eight years can be characterized as a shadow democracy. Intolerance in the deceptive guise of political correctness, racial hatred camouflaged as striving for a more perfect world in which social justice and universal human rights would finally triumph, were the memes du jour. The "Never Trump" movement has grown out of this milieu, in which noble slogans have been mixed with blind hatred and political ambitions have turned into poison pills by the self-appointed champions of social justice and biased notions of human rights.

The elevation of the death of George Floyd, a hardened career criminal to the status of a black hero, has only deepened the gulf between the races in American society. As so many times before in American history, the soul-killing notion of victimhood has been combined with the raising of racial hatred and revenge to the highest pedestal of ultimate cultural vision of the African American community. These entrenched destructive syndromes have manifested themselves most blatantly by the intellectually impaired and politically incompetent rant of the Mayor of Chicago Lori Lightfoot when she addressed the President thus: "I have one thing to say to President Trump: It starts with F and ends with U." To wit, no one within the Democrat Party nor a single journalist in the media admonished the Mayor that her outburst did not further decent discourse in American politics. Moreover, this blooming idiot made her statement immediately following the murder of 18 black people in a single day in her city.

Yet, Lori Lightfoot has not been alone. Senator Spartacus, an embarrassment for New Jersey as well as to every intelligent individual, wants to punch the President in the face. Joe Biden the Superman is ready to physically beat up the President. Congresswoman Maxine Waters, the pride of California, encourages the mob to harass Trump supporters. Jimmy Kimmel, another black face darling and a hypocritical friend of the black community, jokes about assassinating the President. Snoop Dog produces a video actually assassinating the President. Kathy Griffin poses with the severed and bloody head of the President. Joining this elite group of idiots, Johnny Depp also jokes about assassinating the President. Madonna is even more "heroic." She wants to blow up the White House. The allegedly peaceful and victimized Black Lives Matter calls for murdering police or, in the alternative, frying them alive. Antifa demands the immediate outbreak of a bloody revolution by regularly insulting the United States of America and every Republican office holder. Congresswoman Rashida Tlaib who considers herself "Palestinian" first, calls the President "Motherfuc**r." And so on and so forth.

On the other side of the aisle, Senator Cotton's case with The New York Times, the canceling of movies such as the classic Gone with the Wind, Drew Brees' apology for calling kneeling during the national anthem disrespectful, the vicious criticism of Ellen DeGeneres' comment about "people of color," and numerous other manifestations of despotic overreactions by African American extremists must worry every American for the democratic future of the nation. Apparently, Voltaire's words have lost their relevance in today's American democracy: "I disapprove of what you say, but I will defend to the death your right to say it."

The urge of destroying the old and replacing it with something new has always been present in American history. However, the so-called "Cancel Culture" has a much more dangerous and sinister objective. Acting like the Bolsheviks in Russia and later in the Soviet Union, and imitating to the fullest the German National Socialists, Black Lives Matter, Antifa, and all the other so-called "anti-fascists" have adopted the ideologies and actions of the Communists and the Fascists. Lenin's thugs destroyed art works, toppled statues, murdered people indiscriminately, in the name of the Proletar Revolution that supposedly were destined to bring about a new and better world. The Nazis's destruction of the so-called "entartete Kunst" - degenerate art -, the burning of books that they disliked, and the consignment of Jews, Gypsies, and their opposition to concentration and annihilation camps, were all planned genocides against the past, the present, and the future of mankind.

History is a collection of facts. One is allowed to like or dislike some, most, or all of those facts. However, history existed for several millennia. The destroyers do not have a time machine to travel back in history and reenact the past to their liking. Moreover, biased and one-sided interpretation of history does not foster unity. On the contrary, it will surely lead to divisions that will ultimately result in the destruction of the Republic. This senseless destruction must not be permitted to continue in the country of freedom and democracy, in the "city on the shining hill," to which all the freedom-loving people have longed to come, in order to partake in the American dream. For these reasons, the idiotic orgy of those extremist organizations must be stopped immediately and decisively, if needed by force. Finally, public and private organizations also must stop submitting to the demands of the extremists, whose goal is to establish a despotic communist regime in the United States of America.

Rather, they should follow Leicester Mayor's stand who refused to give in to the Black Lives Matters' demand to tear down the statue of Mahatma Gandhi. Quite disingenuously this movement declared Gandhi a "fascist, racist, and sexual predator." Mayor Sir Peter Soulsby of the English town demurred and stated that he had no intention of removing the statue. Residents of the town formed a protective circle around the statue and were joined by their elected representatives. Sir Peter said: "There is no prospect at all of us removing it. And I'm not sure we'd have the power to take it down anyway. It was a community effort to put it there to celebrate some-one who, for all of us, was very inspirational leader in India who inspired the rest of the world with this creed of non-violence." American politicians on both sides of the aisle and confused businessmen should follow the example of Sir Peter to the letter. History does not exist to only serve an ideologically drunk minority. History is not there to be expropriated and monopolized by Black Lives Matter and like-minded organizations. History belongs to everybody, because it includes mankind without the haphazard vagaries of racial discrimination.

The world's eyes are fixated on America. Its allies watch with mount-ing concerns and its foes celebrate with rising malicious joy. On November 3, 2020, Americans must choose between destruction and construction. Be-tween a United States of America where the military is ignored, the police is defunded, private property is disrespected, personal freedom is eliminated, and democracy is ridiculed - and a flourishing economy, a strong military, an effective police force, and a democracy, in which law and order prevails, indi-vidual rights are protected, and law abiding people can go about their business without fear of the lawless mob's barbarous terror. The casualty list of this destructive spirit must include foreign relations as well as national security.

After all, the United States of America is still the richest and the most powerful state on earth. Yet, it is also deeply divided. The protests, riots, and mayhem have brought about a national tragedy. What is even more serious, unity is out of reach in the near future. Could a coherent foreign policy fashioned and conducted succeed without having a broad consensus about the main principles of national interests? Stability and peace are two constructs that have been breaking down for at least the last three decades in the world. Is it in the interest of the United States of America to further jeopardize these two pillars of a crumbling world order?

What if, after the November elections, the sole superpower would con-tinue to be partially paralyzed by internal upheavals? Moreover, what if American-Chinese relations would take a turn to the worse? Furthermore, what if the Libya conflict would trigger an all consuming explosion in the greater Middle Middle East, North Africa, and South-East Asia? Finally, what if the People's Republic of China's relentlessly aggressive expansionist policies should lead to a collusion among the Asian states, primarily with

India, Japan, Vietnam, Indonesia, the Philippines, and Australia? Could the United States of America take upon itself the responsibility of not being prepared or not doing everything in its powers to prevent multiple explosions in at least three continents?

Clearly, the United States of America is in dire need to have a President with indisputable qualities of leadership. Leadership that is able to be contrarian when needed, but possesses the intellect to convince the majority to follow when it is required. A leader who is not detached from realities and is equipped with humanity and culture to unite the successive generations in patriotic fervor. A President who knows the world as well as the limits within which a superpower should confine itself to avoid national ruin and global destruction.

Among these factors, managing the American-Chinese rivalry is the most important matter in the bilateral as well as in the global contexts. In the middle of COVID-19, cool-headed reasoning must prevail. Even before the outbreak of the COVID-19 pandemic, the People's Republic of China has begun regressing politically, economically, financially, and culturally. Politically, President Xi's reenactment of Mao's personal cult has paralyzed even constructive dialogues and debate within the ruling gremium of the Chinese Communist Party. His hubristic megalomania has created multiple problems for the latter domestically as well as internationally.

Economically, the dangerous accumulation of state debts has made the country the most debt-ridden in the world. Meanwhile, the Chinese economy has been struggling with the accelerated aging of the population, due to Mao's one child policy. This demographic handicap has been the cause of a steep decline in productivity. Moreover, the economy entered in 2007, an irreversible regression era, in which a very rapid deceleration in growth has stymied expansion. Finally, to conceal these negative trends, the leadership has embarked on an expedited campaign of excessive reliance on capital investment, especially in infrastructure. To make matters worse, the government has increased consumer and industrial spending by indiscriminately extending available credit. The result has been the piling up of debt and a precipitous decline of China's GDP from double digits annual growth to single digit drop. These two contravening trends do not bode well for the long term political durability of the Chinese Communist Party.

Financially, China is at the center of a middle income trap. Wages in the cities situated along the Pacific east coast are rising, while standard of living in the interior remains stagnant or are in decline. As a result, tensions between these two poles have steadily been rising. Ironically, the middle class has been shrinking too, because of the astronomical prices for housing and other assets for the individual Chinese.

Culturally, President Xi and the party he heads maneuvered China into another cul de sac. By opening the middle class' horizon, albeit through a barely cracked virtual door, simultaneously to Western culture and Confucius' teachings, President Xi unintentionally has weakened the Chinese "heavenly harmony" between the Communist Party's despotism and the Western and Confucian notion of individual freedoms.

To add a final insult to countless injuries, President Xi is keen to hide his country's rapidly mounting domestic problems behind nationalistic and racist rhetoric fueled aggressive foreign expansion. Today, the People's Republic of China's foreign policy is characterized by oriental harmony between brute reason and brute force. As Mao Tse-tung explained long ago: "In reasoning we shall start by delivering shock and yelling at the patient, you are sick, so that he is scared into a sweat, and then we will tell him gently that he needs treatment." The "treatment" consists, according to Mao, of applying brute force to annihilate anyone who happens to disagree with any Chinese dictum.

Clearly, the lesson that Mao drew from the historic humiliation of Imperial China in the hands of several foreign powers in the 19th and early 20th centuries was that their "brute force" should be avenged by an even stronger Communist Chinese "brute force." The latter's manifestations in political and military terms are clearly apparent in the rapidly escalating global and regional hostility of Beijing toward its Asian neighbors and the rest of the world. President Xi's strategic roadmap is an audacious attempt to turn Mao's vision into reality. The main vehicle of the People's Republic's resurgence is the attempted revival of the historic "Silk Road," dubbed by the Communists as the "One Belt One Road" initiative. This lofty initiative, announced by President Xi in 2013, in Kazakhstan, and revised in March 2015, in a major speech delivered by him personally, is reminiscent of the vocabulary used by the Han and Tang dynasties in their apex. The slogan

"One Belt" is an allusion to the land route encompassing Central Asia, Russia and Europe. The term "One Road" is grossly misleading, because it connotes a maritime route through the Pacific and Indian Oceans.

Appropriately, albeit confusingly, the National Development and Reform Commission, China's powerful central planning organization, published a voluminous document, entitled "Visions and Actions on Jointly Building Silk Road Economic Belt and 21st century Maritime Silk Road." Despite its size, the document entails few details about the implementation of President Xi's grand vision. Yet, it ominously refers to a "security component," meaning a greater regional and global role of the security apparatus and the military.

Prior to the aggressive construction of artificial islands' fortresses in the disputed waters of the East and South China Sea, the People's Republic of China did not possess foreign military bases. Disingenuously, Beijing adamantly insists that the Spratly Islands, an assortment of Reefs as far south as Malaysia, the Senkaku Islands, belonging to Japan, in the north, and named the Diaoyutai Islands by the Republic of China, are within its "indisputable sovereignty." According to this Chinese claim, it's alleged "sovereignty" covers an area more than twice the size of the Gulf of Mexico. In actuality, this claim is absolutely illegal and based solely on a forgery, namely, a recently miraculously discovered map, allegedly prepared in 1947 by the Nationalist Government of Chiang Kai Shek. This lawless Chinese policy harks back to two ancient Chinese principles. The first is the command of "Dah, dah! Tahn, tahn! Dah, dah!" - meaning "Fight for a while; talk for a while; fight again!" The second principle is Sun Tzu's advice that "supreme excellence consists in breaking the enemy's resistance without fighting."

Unfortunately, for decades, successive American governments have pursued policies of appeasement, instead of decisive opposition, in response to Beijing's use of "Brute Force." Erroneously, American policymakers have asserted that economic cooperation coupled with technological assistance will remove the appeal of the remnants of Maoism and communist ideology. In reality, while Chinese leaders have welcomed foreign investment and know how, it has become abundantly obvious that large scale penetration of the Chinese market has raised the political red flag about opening the floodgates to foreign economic dominance - and by implication, to political influence.

Given the old Chinese virtues of patience and deviousness, combined with Beiging's cyber warfare capabilities, President Xi and his colleagues are about to try constructing a new world order. The contours of their new empire eerily resembles Mao Tse-tung's expansionist dreams. In a conversation with the late Anna Louise Strang he explained to her his theory of "an intermediate zone." In it, the United States of America was the supreme enemy. As in his subsequent writings, he listed the countries that he considered to be either Chinese territory or dependent states, seized through unequal treaties by the so-called imperialist powers. Those are: Burma, Bhutan, Sikkim, Nepal, Hong Kong, Korea, the Republic of China (Taiwan), the Pescadores, the Ryukyu Islands of Japan, outer Mongolia, the entire Indochina, and Macau. Mao dismissed the validity of the Aigun Treaty of 1858, and the ILI Treaty of 1881, with Tsarist Russia. Accordingly, Mao insisted that Kazakhstan, Kirghizia, Tadjikistan, and the whole of Siberia are part of the "sacred motherland of the Chinese People's Republic."

In this context, very little attention is paid in Washington, D.C. and in the other capitals to the strategic role that the so-called "overseas Chinese," the hua chiao, have played in Beijing's expansionist design. Economically dominant across Asia and with their belief that they belong to a superior civilization and the dominant race, they resist assimilation into the societies and cultures of their host countries. Regardless of their eventual disdain for the political regime in Beijing, their loyalty is firmly anchored in their ancestral motherland. No wealth, political status, or appeasement will move them away from this umbilical cord expressed in the following passionate words: "Wo shih Kou jen! Wo chu tsai Nanyang! Wo ai Chung Kuo!" "I am Chinese! I live in the Southern Ocean! I love China!"

Xi Jinping is the reincarnation of both Stalin and Mao. He is a ruthless dictator. The sooner the rest of the world demonstrates the folly of his lawless and aggressive behavior, the more peaceful and stable Asia and the rest of the world will be. President Xi and his colleagues must also realize that their policies will not lead to dominance but to failure and defeat. The challenge for President Trump and his administration is to impress credibly upon President Xi the ultimate consequences of their reckless "Brute Reason," and "Brute Force" policies.

The chief strategic interests of the United States of America in the

Pacific theatre are twofold. First, to uphold the principle of Freedom of Navigation Operations (FONOP) that is codified in Article 87 (1) of the 1982 United Nations Convention on the Law of the Sea. Accordingly, the principle means "freedom of movement for vessels, freedom to enter ports and to make use of plants and docks, to load and unload goods and to transport goods and passengers." Indisputably, Chinese claims to large areas of the South China Sea, its land reclamations, its artificial expansion of those islets and reefs, as well as its militarization of the illegally occupied lands, are unambiguously in violation of international law. In contravention to their international legal obligations, Beijing points to two obscure Chinese legal acts: The Law of the People's Republic of China on the Territorial Sea and the Contiguous Zone and the Declaration of the Government of the People's Republic of China on the Baselines of the Territorial Sea.

The list of American, Australian, and Japanese FONOP activities are very long. These naval operations and flyovers must be maintained. In addition, any Chinese intransigence must be countered decisively and with overwhelming force.

The second chief strategic interest of the United States of America is to ensure that its allies know that they can count on its unequivocal support against any Chinese belligerence. The most recent hostilities between China and India in the Galwan Valley high up in the disputed Himalayan border region should be a warning sign to every state on the continent. In this case, Beijing has been laying claim to the area for decades. The deadly confrontation in the Galwan Valley, part of the Ladakh region along the long Himalayan frontier between the two Asian giants, was the deadliest in almost five decades. According to Indian sources 20 Indian and 48 Chinese soldiers were killed.

For strategic clarity, the Galwan Valley is situated in a remote stretch of the 2,100-mile long Line of Actual Control, so named after the border established following a war between India and China in 1962 that resulted in an uneasy truce. As a footnote, then Prime Minister of India Jawaharlal Nehru who trusted then Chinese Prime Minister Zhou Enlai under the Five Principles of Peaceful Coexistence, also known as the Panchsheel or Panch Shila Agreement, was completely unprepared and gravely disappointed by the Chinese belligerence that culminated in a defeat of the Indian military by the Chinese People's Liberation Army. It is noteworthy to remark that the first codification of these principles in a bilateral treaty form was in an agreement between China and India in 1954. The five principles, as stated in this treaty, were listed as: 1. Mutual respect for each other's territorial integrity and sovereignty; 2. Mutual non-aggression; 3. Mutual non-interference in each other's internal affairs; 4. Equality and mutual benefit; and 5. Peaceful coexistence.

In the same vein, India's current Prime Minister Narendra Modi also expressed his "hurt and anger" about the latest Chinese aggression. Meanwhile, Chinese Foreign Ministry spokesman Zhao Lijian said that "the Galwan Valley is located on the Chinese side of the Line of Actual Control in the west section of the China-India boundary." This statement, as so many similar Chinese assertions, is blatantly false. To illustrate the point, the valley comprises a land area between steep mountains that buffet the Galwan River. The river originates in Aksai Chin, on the Chinese side of the Line of Actual Control, but flows into the Shyok River on the Indian side. The Line of Actual Control lies east of the confluence of the two rivers that is jointly patrolled by both countries. Until the June 15, 2020 clashes, Chinese maps have shown that the Chinese side of the Line of Actual Control ends short of the confluence of the two rivers. This fact corresponds with India's understanding of the demarcation line. By wrongly claiming that the entire valley is on the Chinese side, Beijing wants to establish a fait-accompli on the ground by military force.

Yet, Chinese aggressive expansionism does not end in the Galwan Valley. Beijing's aggressive stand in the South as well as the East China Sea has claimed the lives of Vietnamise, Philippino, Japanese, and Malaysian fishermen. President Xi also regularly threatens the Republic of China (Taiwan) by using rude language in marked departure from his previous and more careful statements. The same observation applies to President Xi's and other high ranking officials' utterances regarding Australia. The Chinese Ambassador to Camberra opined that Australia is nothing but chewing gum stuck to the Chinese shoe sole. With the COVID-19 pandemic wreaking havoc across the globe, President Xi is determined to facilitate as many territorial gains as possible and make China the undisputed hegemon of the Asian continent.

This Chinese strategic aggression by military force implies that Beijing made up its mind to rule or to ruin. Its disregard for international law, its contempt for the rights of other nations, its intolerance toward opposing viewpoints, and its one-sided globalist vision, should be a red flag for the rest of the world. Every nation should realize that the present international order is in danger and must be saved from Beijing. The multiple fires that President Xi and his colleagues have unleashed on the world must be snuffed out with unity of purpose against their hubristic adventurism.

Such a unified stand against the People's Republic of China is needed not just among the United States of America and its Asian partners, but also among member states of NATO and Washington, D.C. and the 27 member states of the European Union. On June 18, 2020, the organization's foreign affairs chief Josep Borrell penned an article published extensively in several European newspapers, in which he expanded on the ambivalent relationship between Beijing and the member states of the European Union. Designating China a "partner country," but warning against not "acting jointly against superpowers," he again proved that the European Union did not choose wisely by electing him to speak on their behalf about international affairs. Placing China and America in the same box, Borrell made clear that his preference is neutrality and not alliance with the United States of America. His main gripe against Beijing is that the Chinese Communist Party politicized its assistance to Europe during the COVID-19 pandemic. "The change in the EU's relations with China has accelerated in different phases since the outbreak of COVID-19. When the hospitals in China were overloaded, the EU provided extensive support without making a fuss about it. Later, when Europe became the epicenter of the pandemic, China sent medical equipment on a large scale and made the world aware of it." In conclusion, he almost sounded apologetic: "The key point is that we should support each other and show international solidarity - and the European Union has always shown how committed it is here - but that we should avoid political capital from such help to beat. (sic)"

Borrell's article appeared on the same day when President Xi held a telephone conversation with Hungarian Prime Minister Viktor Orban, in which the Chinese leader affirmed his support for the "United Nations and World Health Organization in fighting the pandemic." Calling Prime Minister Orban by President Xi was not a coincidence. The latter and some of his colleagues from the former Soviet Bloc have benefited mightily of Chinese largesses, which were clearly designed as corrupting bribes to split the member states of the European Union. Yet, the appeasement of Beijing has not stopped with the East European states. Greece, Italy, France, and Spain, the soft underbelly of Europe have also been fairly susceptible to Chinese corruption.

Additional remarks by the aforementioned Mr. Borrell are even more unhelpful. Speaking in front of a group of German diplomats on May 25, 2020, Mr. Borrell, never shy to show off his strategic brilliance, mused thus: "Analysts have long talked about the end of an American-led system and the arrival of an Asian century. This is now happening in front of our eyes." For good measure, he added that the coronavirus pandemic could be seen as a turning point and that the "pressure to choose sides is growing." Alluding to the long-standing alliance with the United States of America, but also trying to sweeten his moronic remarks, he said that the 27 member states "should follow our own interests and values and avoid being instrumentalized by one or the other." With Mr. Borrell at the helm of the European Union's foreign policy, all member states should rest assured that he would bring European and Chinese values into perfect heavenly harmony.

Mr. Borrell's reluctance to see the People's Republic of China for what it really is does not sit well with other commissioners of the European Union. Margrethe Vestager, the competition head and , therefore, a key figure in how the organization will manage the China relations, has criticized the lack of reciprocity: "In the part of West Denmark, in which I grew up, we were taught that if you invite a guest to dinner and they do not invite you back, you stop inviting them." She added that Europe needed "to be more assertive and confident about who we are." Clearly, Mr. Borrell's naivete toward Beijing and his visible dislike of America are not an effective combination for the European Union in its quest to formulate a coherent policy toward the People's Republic of China. His new pseudo-realism would lead the organization into a global subservient relationship with President Xi and his Chinese Communist Party.

The slanted European perspective is in full display by Andrew Small's comments who happens to be a senior fellow at the European Council on Foreign Relations. Talking about the errors in European judgement toward

China he said: "It (China) benefited from the contrast that many Europeans drew between China and Russia. In this view, whereas Russia was actively hostile to the EU, China only sought to stymie European unity on a set of narrowly Sincentric issues; whereas Russia thrived on chaos, China could be relied on as a status quo actor during crises; and whereas Russia pumped out disinformation, targeted European citizens, and sought to bring populists to power, China focused on positive image management and behind-the-scenes elite capture." With friends like these, does America need enemies?!

Yet, disagreements between the United States of America and the European Union do not stop with the People's Republic of China. The bone of contention is Israel's plans to annex Jewish settlements in the West Bank of the Jordan River. Leading the chorus of the anti-annexation states, French Foreign Minister Jean-Yves Le Drian stated that partial annexation of the West Bank and the Jordan Valley by Israel would be considered a "serious violation" by Paris. Naturally, Josep Borrell also chimed in. He announced that Brussels would work to "discourage any possible initiative toward annexation," a policy approach totally at odds with the White House's view, which leaves the decision up to Jerusalem. As in so many times in the past, Mr. Borrel also ran afoul of the majority of the member states, in particular Austria and Hungary. In a letter addressed to Mr. Borrel, they called upon the EU foreign policy chief to reconvene the EU-Israel Association Council, which is the official framework for ministerial-level dialogue between the European Union and Israel. In this letter, the member states urged Mr. Borrell to strengthen and not weaken ties with Israel. The signatories, headed by Antonio Lopez-Isturiz White of Spain, chairman of the European parliament Delegation for Relations with Israel, called upon Mr. Borrell to resuscitate the since 2012 dormant council as an "effective forum for close dialogue and consultation" in light of the current "pressing challenges and significant shared interests" between Brussels and Jerusalem.

A more serious challenge to American foreign policy has come for decades from the Turkish President Recep Tayyip Erdogan, who termed Israel's partial annexation "further theft" of Palestinian land. With Turkey and Egypt close to a military confrontation over Libya, President Erdogan is using the annexation issue to further bolster his image in the Muslim world as a fundamentalist Muslim and an uncompromising supporter of the Palestinian cause. His fierce anti-Semitic and anti-Israeli rhetoric could force

Egyptian President Abdel Fattah al-Sisi to take a more hardline approach toward Israel. This, in turn, would force the United Arab Emirates and the Kingdom of Saudi Arabia to follow suit.

The member states of the Arab League as well as the six monarchies of the Gulf Consultative Council (GCC) have been severely affected by the double whammy of COVID-19 and the shrinking demand for oil and gas. Since the Middle East is strategically important as a commercial bridge between Asia and Europe, the United States of America cannot remain oblivious to the instability of the region. Combined with the mounting challenges in Europe, America cannot afford the domestic turmoil and the Democrats intransigence for long. In this manner, oscillating among three major challenges, Asia, Europe, and the greater Middle East, American foreign policy might be consigned to a vacuum. For paralysis will result in a bottomless vacuum of indecisions, obfuscations, and the loss of great power status. A dreadful possibility for the United States of America, because its domestic as well as foreign powers would not rest on credible and solid foundations.

When the Soviet Union ceased to exist and Russia emerged as its successor state, leaders across the European Union believed, as their soulmates on the other side of the Atlantic Ocean, that there will be a miraculous epiphany in the Kremlin and the entire continent will march in unison toward the post- Cold War world of democracy, market economy, and rule of law. As in Washington, D.C., the politicians and bureaucrats in Brussels were convinced that they were destined to teach and lead Russia in its path to a Westernized nation. Both President Yeltsin and Foreign Minister Kozyrev thought that a well-defined partnership with NATO and the European Union would be beneficial for Russia's future developments. President Yeltsin went even further by stating that the West is Russia's "ally in the common struggle against the Soviet system."

To follow up on this developing partnership, the European Union and Russia signed the Partnership and Cooperation Agreement (PCA) in 1994, a framework that still serves as the legal framework for their relations. The PCA is based on the "respect for democratic principles and human rights as an essential element of the partnership" and Russia's commitment to "support efforts to consolidate its democracy, develop its economy, and complete the transition into a market economy." Meanwhile, because of the war in Chechnya, the PCA only entered into force in 1997. This legalistic approach of quid pro quo was interpreted in the Kremlin as illegitimate meddling in its internal affairs. Hence, the distancing of Russia from the West began. The beginning of Putin's presidency heralded the shift to a more pronounced Euroasian strategy and a corresponding Euroasian identity. This shift, in turn, was practically the death knell of the PCA.

Brussels' second attempt at closer cooperation occurred in 2005, at the St. Petersburg summit. As a result, the European Union and Russia have begun working toward the establishment of four "Common Spaces" to define a more detailed framework for mutual cooperation. With the blessing of the United States of America, economic relations, freedom, security, and justice; external security, and research and development were selected as the main components of broad based cooperation.

The launching of Brussels' Eastern Partnership (ENP) initiative in 2009, was viewed in Moscow as another hostile attempt to intrude upon Russia's red line of "near abroad," also called by President Putin "Russia's sphere of influence" and "Russia's privileged interests." Comprising Armenia, Azerbaijan, Belarus, Georgia, Moldova, and Ukraine, with the objective of bringing them closer to the European Union, the ENP's ultimate goal was to deepen cooperation and integration of these states based on European Union values, norms, and standards. The Kremlin's answer came in the form of an invasion of Georgia, followed by sanctions imposed by the West and most of the member states of the United Nation.

Again, the Kremlin countered in 2011, with its own initiative, dubbed the Euroasian Custom Union (ECU). In addition, the strategic back-and-forth coincided with the eastward expansion of NATO. Reacting to the inclusion of the Baltic states and the Central and East European states into NATO, Russian Foreign Minister Lavrov stated: "Our Western partners chose…(to expand) NATO eastward and (to move) the geopolitical space under their control closer to Russia's border. This is the root cause of the systemic problems that affect Russia's relations with the United States and Europe."

The European Union's relations with Russia have become even more tense since Russia's annexation of the Crimea in 2014. The Kremlin's support for the Russian ethnic minority in eastern Ukraine further increased tensions between the former and the latter. Brussels, as Washington, D.C., strongly condemned Russia's violation of Ukraine's sovereignty and territorial integrity. Expressing the Kremlin's strong objection to the planned Association Agreement with Ukraine, President Putin defended his country's actions thus: "...with Ukraine, our western partners have crossed the line.... They must have really lacked political instinct and common sense not to foresee all the consequences of their actions. Russia found itself in a position it could not retreat from. If you compress the spring all the way to its limit, it will snap back hard." Russia's understanding of itself as still a military superpower collided with the United States of America's and the European Union's joint vision of being the more mature side in an uneasy relationship.

In view of these two conflicting images of themselves, Russia's militarism will override other considerations. Its "Realpolitik" will remain devoid of nostalgia or human emotions. No poverty or financial misfortune of its citizenry will appeal successfully to alter the course of military buildup and the repeated use of row force. Moscow's military involvements in Syria and Libya attest to this elementary conclusion. The West must understand that the main evil of Putin's Russia is that it is soaked in total dissoluteness and will never adhere to legal principles, because it has emancipated itself from the rule of law, both internally as well as externally.

X. A Personal Perspective

Human beings are prone to succumb to lies when their minds are disorderly, their thinking is unsettled, and their hearts are hungry for affection. Living with lies condemns the person to lead an artificial existence, in which the truth incapacitates his or her judgment. Knowing that I was lied to turned out to be the worst feeling that I experienced in the first decade on my young earthly existence.

I was born in Hungary, amidst the height of the reign of the Little Stalin, as Matyas Rakosi the then Hungarian Communist tyrant was called, in a town that has proudly displayed its designation of being the "Famous City." My family was well-known in Kecskemet. Before World War II, my paternal grandfather owned the only slaughterhouse in town and most of the apartment buildings along the main street. After World War II, my father headed the gynecology department of the county hospital and was a well-liked physician with a golden heart. Clearly, I was born into privilege. Isolated from the ubiquitous misery and taught in school that Communist Hungary was already an earthly paradise, I believed my teachers' lies. The October 23, 1956 Revolution changed my early life.

My epiphany came at the age of 10 when my father was allowed by the Hungarian government to accept a medical position in Israel. We spent four years in a country in which the pioneering spirit of building a new state for the people who were persecuted for two millennia and barely survived the holocaust was at its height. The sheer enthusiasm and the all pervasive feeling of national unity were overwhelming. In those four years, I became an unadulterated devotee of democracy. With my new friends I attended many campaign events. For me to hear that the then Prime Minister David ben Gurion, also affectionately called the Father of Israel, was regularly dubbed as a cheat, a crook, a criminal, and even worse, by his political opponents was a real eye opener. At that time, there was a widely circulating joke in Israel. It went like this: Three Rabbis are sitting at the same table in a cafe house. In Israel everybody knew that in the entire country there are no three Rabbis who would sit in agreement around the same coffee table. Yet, in spite of their strong disagreements about almost everything, no Israeli citizen supported anti-democratic views, advocated economic and social policies that were hostile to the teachings of the Torah, the Talmud, and the traditions of the Jewish Nation. Judaism as a religion was the key to the strength and the well-being of the nation. Religious unity, in turn, created a strong sense of political confidence.

At the age of 15, my family and I returned to Hungary. For me the place was a human cemetery. Instead of boisterous self-confidence, lively political and social surroundings, and freedoms, Communist Hungary was lacking even the semblance of national confidence and freedoms. At first, I tried to lead a life that I got used to in Israel. After having been kicked out of three high schools for speaking the truth to my teachers, I learned to shut up. I started to lead a schizophrenic life. In my solitary loneliness, I wanted to leave Hungary as soon as I could. In my public existence, I held my tongue. Still, due to my being the son of an intellectual, I had difficulties to be accepted to the prestigious School of Political and Legal Sciences at the Eotvos Lorand University in Budapest. The university was full of the children of the Communist "affirmative action" that did not earn their admission on merit. Accordingly, children of Workers and Peasants and the children of those who "fought" for the government, were accepted almost automatically, while the descendants of the so-called intelligentsia, considered to be hostile to the regime, could only be admitted if their parents had so-called "social connections," also dubbed "protekcio" in Hungarian. Its English equivalent is favoritism. Luckily, through my father, I had a high ranking official who was willing to intercede on my behalf.

Following my graduation, I was assigned to the Prosecutor's Office in my hometown. Having taken the state exam for judges and prosecutors with distinction within half of the time allocated to the obligatory legal apprenticeship, I was transferred to Budapest. The three years that I spent with the Fourth Branch of government gave me an in-depth look at the working of the one-party dictatorship.

The following January, I successfully escaped Hungary. After four years in Germany, I was offered a job in Washington, D.C. with a research unit of the U.S. Congress. As a new citizen, I was detailed to the Reagan White House and the Supreme Court of the United States of America in quick succession. Based on my life experiences, I love this country unconditionally. I am deeply appreciative of being an American citizen and that my children and my grandchildren can live in a free country. As far as my country of birth is concerned, it has still not recovered from the disease of the Soviet invented Communist/Socialist nightmare. In my opinion, Hungary remains beyond redemption.

The lesson I personally learned from these experiences is summarized succinctly by Matthew 7:24-27. "Anyone who listens to my teaching and follows it is wise, like a person who builds a house on solid rock. Though the rain comes in torrents and the floodwaters rise and the winds beat against that house, it won't collapse because it is built on bedrock. But anyone who hears my teaching and doesn't obey it is foolish, like a person who builds a house on sand. When the rains and floods come and the winds beat against the house, it will collapse with a mighty crash."

Indeed, the bedrock upon which the United States of America has been built is its traditional and timeless Judeo-Christian ethos. Clearly, this ethos is under relentless attack by a minority that would want to see the foundation of the Republic collapse. Among the countless unconstitutional attempts to annihilate the Judeo-Christian governance, the most outrageous is the Kansas City ordinance by Mayor Quinton Lucas, a Democrat, who ordered pastors to turn over the names, addresses, and phone numbers of anyone who enters church houses. The ordinance says: "Religious gatherings, including but not limited to, weddings, funerals, memorial services, and wakes, of ten persons inside or ten percent of building occupancy (whichever number is greater) and fifty people outside may resume, provided social distancing is maintained and event organizers maintain a record of attendees." Thus, under the guise of fighting the spread of COVID-19, Mayor Lucas feels entitled to violate the constitutional principle of separation of state and church, and impose measures only employed until now by despotic regimes elsewhere but not in the United States of America. And he is not alone. Democrat governors and mayors across the land have been abusing their rights under the pandemic to radically transform the country to their small-minded, secular image.

Hawk Newsome, who chairs Black Lives Matter of Greater New York, argued that because violence and rioting appeared to be getting the point across more effectively, those actions were justifiable. Thus, telling the overwhelming majority by a small minority how to live and what and how to think is proper in a democracy. This "the ends justify the means" mentality is self-obsessed, arrogant, and devoid of any tolerance or empathy. Essentially, Mr. Newsome in his self-righteousness has declared that the mob and the thugs have the right to rule illegally over the majority. Accordingly, he expressed his intention to "shove legislation down people's throats." Overpowered by raw emotions that have clearly befogged his intellect, he intoned: "If this country doesn't give us what we want then we will burn down the system and replace it." What Mr. Newsome and his comrades-in-arms want the absolute power of a despotic minority. Then, drunk with this power, they will destroy everything, including themselves, because they do not have the faintest idea of what the replacement should be or how to govern at all.

To wit, the Los Angeles chapter of Black Lives Matter demanded the resignation of the County District Attorney Jackie Lacey, an African American and card-carrying radical liberal, for failing to prosecute more police officers who were involved in fatal shootings during her tenure in office. Melina Abdullah, one of the co-founders of the city's Black Lives Matter chapter, castigated District Attorney Lacey for not taking more cases to court. Her complaint is outrageous. On the one hand, she is not even superficially familiar with those cases. On the other hand, she was neither elected nor appointed to the position Ms. Lacey currently occupies. For Ms. Abdullah, talking more than listening, playing the victim, treating others who disagree with her disparagingly, criticizing everybody without factual basis, and employing lies to support her false narrative, are justified in the name of political correctness paired with racial wrath.

The case of Chanelle Helm is even more extreme. Co-Founder of Black Lives Matter, she demands that White people should transfer all their properties to the descendants of slaves, allegedly in the name of social justice. "White people, if you don't have any descendants, will you property to a black or brown family. Preferably one that lives in generational poverty." In her article of August 17, 2017, she laid out 10 "requests to " "White People." Among these gems are some that are more idiotic than the rest. Number 7 states: "White people, especially white women (because this is yaw speciality - Noesy Jenny and Meddling Kathy), get a racist fired. Yaw know what the fuck they be saying. You are complicit when you ignore them. Get your boss fired cause they racist too." Furthermore: "Backing up No. 7, this should be easy but all those sheetless Klan, Nazi's and Other lil' dick-white men will all be returning to work. Get they ass fired. Call the police even: they look suspicious." Then the following: "OK, backing up No. 8, if any white person at your work, or as you enter in spaces and you overhear a white person praising the actions for yesterday, first, get a pic. Get their name and more info. Hell, find out where they work - Get Them Fired. But certainly address them, and, if you need to, you got hands: use them." Moreover: "Commit to two things: Fighting white supremacy where and how you can (this doesn't mean taking up knitting, unless you're making scarves for black and brown kids in need) and funding black and brown people and their work."

A fine example of anti-racist sentiments can be found in the writings of another con-founder of the Black Lives Matter movement. Ms. Yusra Khogali, a Sudanese refugee and proud Marxist, believes that white people are "subhuman" and should be "wiped out." To demonstrate her Marxist compassion, in one of her tweets, by now mercifully deleted, she begged "Allah" to give her the strength not to "kill white people." According to The National Pulse, the deleted tweet said verbatim the following: "Plz Allah give me the strength to not cuss/kill these men and white folks out here today. Plz plz plz." As behooves a genuine "anti-racist" and an expert in medical sciences, which she is not, she opines that white people possess "recessive genetic defects" and should be "wiped out." Moreover, on her Facebook page she asserts that "whiteness is not humxness" and "white skin is sub-humxn." For her insightful comments like these, she received a Canadian government-sanctioned "Young Women in Leadership Award" in 2018.

A dearth of boundaries in decency invites disrespect. The Black Lives Matter movement and its adherents have failed to understand from the movement's inception that their sole focus on what they want has made them lose sight of what they have earned and have deserved. Just taking property arbitrarily by force from those who earned it is unacceptable in a society governed by the rule of law.

Another "gaslighting" of these extremists' and out-of-bound idiots' demand is that in education African Americans should not be required to meet the standards required from White students. According to this self-defeating ultimatum, African American's are not as smart as Whites and, therefore, in the name of racial justice, they should be discriminated against. Advocating the dumbing down of education is tantamount to relegating the United States of America to a second grade status in the world. Employing reverse racism in the age of a new technological revolution, namely, the dawn of the Artificial Intelligence (AI) era, demonstrates that she and her comrades in their intellectual misery cannot even grasp the elementary currents in to-day's world. The utter idiocy of such an assertion is too obvious to further elaborate on.

In a different setting, there is agreement over the dictum that mental patients cannot run the asylum. For this reason alone, this idiocy of a tiny minority of the African American community must be stopped decisively now. The Black Lives Matter, Antifa, and like-minded movements are like cancers inside a healthy body. If these spiritual cancers are allowed to me-tastasize, the United States of America and the rest of the world would face a bleak future.

In order to prevent such an outcome, the following must be done with-out any undue delay. Historically, culture in general and political culture in particular is the product of national and international efforts and collective memory. American political culture is founded on the Declaration of Inde-pendence, the Constitution, and the 240 years institution of the rule of law. Created by a long line of very capable individuals who loved their country, they relied on their faith to address and overcome many challenges. This unique power of culture has propelled the United States of America to greatness and sustained it through many tribulations and tragedies. History cannot be eradicated at the whims of a badly educated and hateful minori-ty. This kind of act would only lead to falsifications and distortions of the heroic story of the nation.

President Trump is absolutely right when he says that defacing and destroying statues and monuments must not be permitted to continue. In George Orwell's prophetic book 1984, Winston Smith regales Julia about the necessity of mind control. "Do you realize that the past, starting from yesterday, has been actually abolished? If it survives anywhere, it's in a few solid objects with no words attached to them, like that lump of glass there." Expanding on this theme, he continues: "Already we know almost literally nothing about the Revolution and the years before the Revolution. Every record has been destroyed or falsified, every book has been rewritten, every picture has been repainted, every statue and street and building has been renamed, every date has been altered. And that process is continuing day by day and minute by minute. History has stopped. Nothing exists except an endless present in which the Party is always right." A nation without history is a people without their existential and spiritual foundation. It absolutely cannot be allowed to happen!

The protesters and the rioters claim, promoted incessantly by the slavish media, that they only want to call attention to the unfair treatment of Blacks, occasioned by the death of George Floyd. Yet, this rhetoric is outrightly false. What they are aiming at is the delegitimization of the United States of America by destroying its past, its present, and its future. Sadly, their destructive strategy has born some fruits. The media apologizes in unison. The academia, Hollywood, Silicon Valley and even Wall Street are going along with the false narrative of "White Supremacy." The hapless and rudderless representatives of the Democrat Party cloaked themselves in the Kente cloth of the Ashanti people of Ghana and kneeled down in self-prostration. Meanwhile, statues of abolitionists are being toppled indiscriminately and monuments fall prey to vandalism.

The African continent is a mess from the Mediterranean Sea to the Indian Ocean. Black Africans are murdering Black Africans by the millions. With rare exceptions, their governments are despotic and corrupt. The people mostly live in extreme poverty and without hope for a better future. Their lives and the lives of African Americans in Democrat-controlled cities and towns do not matter? Or protesting and rioting on their behalf would turn the currently fashionable narrative on its head? Or that they do not want to harmonize the ugly and the uglier features of their destructive crusade against the United States of America? Be as it may, Black Lives Matter and the other like-minded movements cannot be identified with any well-meaning and constructive opposition.

Clearly, it will be a gross dereliction of duty for the overwhelming majority to allow these lawless vandals and terrorists to destroy the country, and with it, the present and the future of successive generations. The harm that they have already inflicted upon the international image of the United

States of America is grave. It has reinforced a false narrative about American society as a heartless and hypocritical entity. As a result, there are military conflicts and political turbulence across the globe. Globally, there are two irreconcilable political thoughts in the world - the democratic and the despotic principles. They are irreconcilable, because these two principles cannot be coupled by superficial concessions or unscrupulous compromises. The forced reconciliation of these two principles within a single country or beyond has already created numerous monster governments worldwide. As the shameful history of Stalin's Soviet Union and Hitler's Germany attested to, a government born of a utopian idea and conceived out of a heap of lies, will always be doomed to a terrific failure. Their reigns were a cavalcade of terror and fear that lit the world on a horrific fire. A power that pretends to be democratic when it is in reality despotism, and a government that pretends to represent the majority when it is not, necessarily becomes corrupt and disgraced. The inevitable outcome of such power is total political and moral collapse.

One could hardly find patriots more committed to the ideals of the United States of America and the rights of the American people than the Founding Father and all the 44 Presidents who succeeded George Washington. Their adherence to equality, the rule of law, and the importance of perfecting American democracy has been unquestionable. For them democracy has meant freedom for all. Slavery was an aberation that has been rectified. African Americans are guaranteed all the rights and the tools to become constructive members of American society. Therefore, the slogans about "systematic racism" and "institutionalized racism" are absolute lies. What should be addressed here in all seriousness is the question about why some of them feel things are going badly for their community? If there is room for improvement, and usually there is, in their political, economic, and cultural developments, appropriate measures should be taken to rectify any shortcoming. However, these measures must be taken within the framework of the rule of law. Under no circumstances should additional emergency legislation be adapted. This terrorist minority cannot move American democracy toward tyrannical legislation. I am sure and I know that the large majority of the American people share my all-encompassing vision of the United States of America's noble past, present, and future that will propel the nation to new heights in the 21st century and beyond.

For me the United States of America is not merely the best country in the world but also symbolizes the mythical bird called the Phoenix of the ancient Greeks and Egyptians. A symbol of renewal and rebirth that, according to the legend, re-emerges from the fire every 500 years. Significantly, only one Phoenix lives at a time. This majestic bird is large and free to soar above the universe as the United States of America has soared and provided hope since its inception to all the oppressed people of the world. Finally, the legendary Phoenix also symbolizes resurrection. Amidst the COVID-19 pandemic, domestic turmoil, and international instability, the American Bald Eagle, like the Phoenix, will rise again to guide the world in the direction of a more just, moral, and equitable future.

Acknowledgement

This book would not have been written without the support of the Testerman family. Bill, Debbie and their daughter Madeleine sheltered me for several months from the possible fatal threat of the coronavirus. Their affection and care went beyond anything I could have expected or imagined. I owe them my highest gratitude.

I also owe a great deal of gratitude to Mary, who read the manuscript on a daily basis and provided me with her perceptive comments that improved the quality of the book.

A special thank you must go to my dear friend Professor Istvan Molnar and his lovely wife Dr. Judit Vadasz for their unrelenting support.

I too would like to thank Goerge Landrith, Chairman and President of the Frontiers of Freedom Institute for his friendship, guidance, and advice throughout our professional and personal affiliation.

Equally, I would like to thank Ruth Holmberg for her editing and guidance that greatly improved the quality of the manuscript.

In addition, I am very thankful for the love that my children and grandchildren bestowed upon me while writing this book. Peter, Judith, Laura, Kailee, Olivia, Alexis, Adriana, Dominic, and Emma Nicole I love you all very much.

Last but not least, I would like to express my deepest appreciation to the United States of America and its citizens for inviting me and my family to become a part of the greatest nation on earth. Knowing that my children, grandchildren, and their descendants will have the privilege to enjoy the blessings of all the rights that the Constitution of this great nation provides without any discrimination to all of its citizens is the most precious blessing I can possess.

About the Author

Miklos K. Radvanyi holds a doctorate in political and legal sciences from the Eotvos Lorand Scientific University in Budapest, Hungary. In addition, he earned a Master's Degree in Comparative Law and American Practice from George Washington University Law School and another Master's degree in International Public Policy from the School of Advanced International Studies, Johns Hopkins University. He authored 6 books in Hungarian, German, and English. He is also the author of over many articles, editorials, and commentaries in three languages. Presently, he is the Senior Executive Vice President of the Frontiers of Freedom Institute in Virginia. He resides in Northern Virginia with his family.